'Christ Lives in Me'

Christmas '81

Dear Marilyn,

Happy Holidays!

Jim & Mary Ann

# 'Christ Lives in Me'

## A Pastoral Reflection on Jesus and His Meaning for Christian Life

Joseph Cardinal Bernardin

Book design and cover by Julie Lonneman.
Cover photographs by James L. Kilcoyne.

SBN 0-86716-044-6

Published by St. Anthony Messenger Press
Printed in the U.S.A.

# Contents

# Foreword

My dear brothers and sisters in Christ:

> The grace of the Lord Jesus Christ, and the love of God,
> and the fellowship of the Holy Spirit be with you all!
> (2 Corinthians 13:13)

I invite you to reflect with me on the most important person in our lives, both as individuals and as a community of faith. That person is Jesus Christ.

I have thought a great deal in recent years about the meaning Jesus has for you, for me and for all men and women. I have also tried to enter into closer communion with the Lord through prayer, so that no part of my life, no part of myself, would be excluded from my relationship with him. This search for union has been an exciting, life-giving experience. But it has brought pain and frustration, too.

Pain, because the closer we are drawn to Jesus, the more conscious we become of our shortcomings and sins. Jesus is the Light of the World. As we approach that Light, it brings ever more sharply into relief the defects in ourselves which we thought, or at least hoped, did not exist!

Frustration, because growth in intimacy with the Lord intensifies my desire to proclaim him and his gospel, and often I feel unequal to the task. There are so many things to do for the Lord, so many people to awaken and encourage, so many initiatives to take. And, more often than not, my efforts fall short of the mark and have little visible effect!

1

Like Paul, I tell myself not to be anxious to see the fruits of the soil I have tilled, for it seems to be of evangelization's very nature that the person who sows the seed is usually not the one who reaps the harvest. Yet I am left with the uneasy feeling that I have not done as much, or done it as well, as the Lord deserved of me.

But I do not despair, and in this, too, I seek to be like Paul. He was so caught up with Jesus, so much in love with him and convinced that his strength was in the Lord, that he never surrendered to discouragement. His many trials only confirmed his faith and strengthened his resolve to preach the gospel to all people, whatever the cost to himself.

As Paul told the Corinthians, "It is not ourselves we preach but Christ Jesus as Lord, and ourselves as your servants for Jesus' sake" (2 Corinthians 4:5). He saw Jesus as a great treasure. So certain was he of Jesus' presence and power in his life, that he could assure the Corinthians without fear or hesitation:

> We are afflicted in every way possible, but we are not crushed; full of doubts, we never despair. We are persecuted but never abandoned; we are struck down but never destroyed. Continually we carry about in our bodies the dying of Jesus, so that in our bodies the life of Jesus may also be revealed. (2 Corinthians 4:8-10)

In that spirit, I want to share with you some of my hopes and aspirations as well as my anxieties and sorrows. I hope these can become for you words of encouragement as you seek to know, love and follow Jesus Christ in the circumstances of your lives. And I ask your prayers for me as I seek to do the same.

# The Importance
# of Christology Today

The *Church* has been the dominant theme of theology in this century, both inside and outside Roman Catholicism. One of the Second Vatican Council's most important documents was the *Dogmatic Constitution on the Church (Lumen Gentium)*.

Perhaps the term for the Church most identified with the Council in Catholics' minds is "People of God." This is a rich biblical image found in both the Old and New Testaments. The Council referred to those baptized into Christ as the "new People of God." It said we are a messianic people:

> Established by Christ as a fellowship of life, charity, and truth, [this people] is also used by him as an instrument for the redemption of all, and is sent forth into the whole world as the light of the world and the salt of the earth (cf. Mt. 5:13-16).[1]

Another important document of the Second Vatican Council is the *Pastoral Constitution on the Church in the Modern World (Gaudium et Spes)*. Whereas *Lumen Gentium* considers the Church's inner nature as established by Christ, *Gaudium et Spes* speaks of how the Church should address the challenges and problems of the concrete temporal situation in which it finds itself. It deals, therefore, with such questions as social and economic justice, war and peace, marriage and culture.

Today, however, the study of Jesus and his meaning for people of our day (Christology) is replacing the study of the

Church (ecclesiology) on center stage. That is logical—perhaps inevitable—for not only was the Church founded by Christ, it is also the Mystical Body of Christ, Christ *present* in the world. To reflect upon the Church leads naturally to reflection upon him.

Furthermore, it seems clear that the internal and external problems and tensions confronting the Church today cannot ultimately be solved on the level of ecclesiology alone. We must have recourse to Christology to understand the inner reality of the Church and to work for its authentic renewal.

This renewed study of Jesus is important to anyone who wants to follow him. To know who *we* are as human beings and as Christians, and to know what it means to live as Christians, we must know who *Christ* is and what meaning his life holds for us. Such knowledge does not come exclusively or even primarily from theology; its best sources are prayer, the sacramental life of the Church and the practice of Christian piety. But theological reflection is also important in deepening and enriching our relationship with Christ.

St. Paul's life and ministry support this view. His letters are rich sources of Christological doctrine. They express the theological reflection on Christ up to that time and carry it dramatically forward. They are crucially important to our own efforts to learn more about Jesus.

Paul's primary intention, however, was not to write a book of theology. He had a simple, practical end in view: to help the early Christians know the Lord better and respond more generously to his expectations, to move them to make Jesus Christ the Lord of their lives.

That is why Paul gave such compelling witness to Jesus' marvelous presence and power in his own life and ministry. Consumed with love for Jesus, Paul found meaning only in the service of his gospel:

> None of us lives as his own master and none of us dies as his own master. While we live we are responsible to the Lord, and when we die we die as his servants. Both in life and in death we are the Lord's. That is why Christ died and came to life again, that he might be Lord of both the dead and the living. (Romans 14:7-9)

Paul's vision lives on today. In *The Redeemer of Man*

4

(*Redemptor Hominis*), the first encyclical of Pope John Paul II, the Holy Father says:

> The Church wishes to serve this single end: that each
> person may be able to find Christ, in order that Christ
> may walk with each person the path of life.... Jesus
> Christ becomes, in a way, newly present, in spite of all his
> apparent absences, in spite of all the limitations of the
> presence and of the institutional activity of the Church.
> Jesus Christ becomes present with the power of the truth
> and the love that are expressed in him with unique
> unrepeatable fullness.... [2]

What does Jesus Christ mean for you and me? What does he offer for our spiritual growth? How does he enrich our understanding of the Church he established and of our role in this community of faith? Where does he fit into our relationships with other people, our evaluation of the critical issues of our times? These are the questions we must consider.

I fervently hope these reflections will help bring us all closer to the Lord Jesus. But any good effect they may have will not finally be due to our efforts, but to Jesus. Finding in us even a small desire to follow him, Jesus is ready to fan our flickering commitment into the flame of an ardent love.

Chapter 1

# The Pastoral Relevance
# of Christology

Christology and Christological dogmas sometimes seem very abstract, to the point that they appear to have little or nothing to do with actual Christian living. Yet Catholic piety and liturgy have always focused on Jesus as the center of Christian life. Now there is a particular need to show how Christological doctrine is equally relevant to our lives as Christians.

A point made in the Introduction bears repeating here. In Christ (and therefore in Christology, which seeks to tell us more about him and his expectations of us) we learn who *we* are and how *we* live. Jesus is our model, and a Christian's life is essentially an "imitation" or "following" of Christ, as we know from Scripture and from our history as a Church.

Peter made this clear on Pentecost, when he addressed the thousands of people in Jerusalem who had witnessed some of the visible manifestations of the Holy Spirit. Having heard Peter's forceful discourse on Jesus' saving deeds and their significance for the human family, the people asked what they were to do. Peter answered: "You must reform and be baptized, each one of you, in the name of Jesus Christ, that your sins may be forgiven" (Acts 2:38).

In other words, Peter was saying: Unite yourselves with the Lord in his death and resurrection and, in doing so, adopt a radically new way of life. We are told that "those who accepted [Peter's] message were baptized; some three thousand were added that day" (Acts 2:41). From that moment on, as they shaped their lives according to the teaching and example of Jesus, they became a "new" people whose values and way of life were recognized as different by their neighbors.

> The community of believers were of one heart and one mind. None of them ever claimed anything as his own; rather, everything was held in common. With power the apostles bore witness to the resurrection of the Lord Jesus, and great respect was paid to them all.
>
> (Acts 4:32-33)

In saying that Jesus is the "model" for Christians, we mean much more than when we say, for example, that Abraham Lincoln, Florence Nightingale, Babe Ruth and Helen Keller are models for young people. People aspire to be "like" other people they admire, but Christians are to be more than just "like" Jesus. They are to *put on* Christ, as Paul told the Corinthians; in a sense, they are to *become* Christ, to be *other* Christs. They are to carry on Christ's work and help bring it to completion.

Although our modeling of Jesus, rooted in union and identification with him, is absolutely central to our lives as Christians, it is exceedingly difficult to explain in human terms. It is unique, part of the Christian mystery which we will never fully comprehend in this life.

Still, some light is shed on it by a common human experience—the process by which members of a family come to resemble one another, psychically as well as physically. This happens not so much by self-conscious imitation, as by a much more profound and organic process involving both genetic factors and personal interaction. We become like those whom we live with and love. As Christians, we are members of God's "family"—adopted sons and daughters of God, brothers and sisters of Christ. And in a real sense we come to resemble Jesus, to be like him, by living with him and loving him.

Jesus himself gave us an image which tells even more about this profound reality:

> "I am the vine, you are the branches.
> He who lives in me and I in him,
> will produce abundantly,
> for apart from me you can do nothing.
> A man who does not live in me

is like a withered, rejected branch,
picked up to be thrown in the fire and burnt." (John 15:5-6)

Plainly this signifies no superficial identification or union. We are affected in our very being—Jesus' life becomes our own. Separated from him, we simply cannot live: We wither spiritually and ultimately die.

Paul understood this; throughout his letters he emphasizes the changes that occur in him as his union with the Lord deepens. He becomes a new creation, his very powerlessness a source of spiritual power because it permits Jesus to work in and through him. So great is this identification that he can say, "... In my own flesh I fill up what is lacking in the sufferings of Christ for the sake of his body, the church" (Colossians 1:24). And to the Galatians: "... the life I live now is not my own; Christ is living in me. I still live my human life, but it is a life of faith in the Son of God, who loved me and gave himself for me" (Galatians 2:20).

What is true of the individual Christian's identification with Jesus is also true for Christians collectively. The Church is Christ's Mystical Body; it is Christ present in the world. It would literally make no sense to separate Christ from the Church and say one accepts the former but rejects the latter.

Further light is shed on these realities when we reflect on the main themes of Christology: for example, on the fact that Jesus is both God and man (the Incarnation); on his redemption of the human family through his death and resurrection; on his triple mission of sanctifying, teaching and governing which continues in and through the Church. Let us consider these themes under two headings: first, the Incarnation and its significance for the human family; second, Jesus as the Way, the Truth and the Life. I shall note the doctrinal points involved, then suggest some of their implications for our lives.

## The Incarnation and Its Significance for the Human Family

Our race is fallen but redeemed; we have glimpsed an eternal destiny. In the heart of every human being is an irrepressible desire for union with the Creator. Not even sin cancels this desire, for even in sinning we still have in view some limited aspect of a good which reflects, however dimly, the perfection of God. Our longing for him does not end, and to suffer eternally this unsatisfied longing is the greatest tragedy imaginable.

Yearning for God was deeply rooted in the Israelites. Despite their disappointments and periodic disloyalty, they never forgot their identity and special dignity as God's people. The human urge to reach out to the Transcendent is beautifully expressed in Psalm 42:

> As the hind longs for the running waters,
>     so my soul longs for you, O God.
> Athirst is my soul for God, the living God.
>     When shall I go and behold the face of God?
> My tears are my food day and night,
>     as they say to me day after day, "Where is your God?"
>                                               (Psalm 42:2-4)

Among the writers of the Christian era, St. Augustine gave particularly poignant expression to this longing. His spiritual pilgrimage and ultimate conversion from a wayward life made him keenly aware of the soul's anguish when it is not in communion with its Lord. "We were made for you, O God," he said, "and our hearts will be restless until they find their rest in you."[3]

It is God who plants this desire in our hearts and God who satisfies it. Conscious as we are of our broken, sinful condition—conscious sometimes even to the point of despairing—we may find this hard to believe. Yet we should not. Having created us in his image and likeness, God loves us so much that he wishes to share his own divine life with us. From the moment humankind first rejected him through sin, he determined to reconcile us with himself, to make us whole again so that we could enjoy the intimacy of his loving friendship. Since then, human history has been at its heart the story of God's self-revelation to his creatures and of our response—faithful at times, unfaithful at other times—to him.

This relationship, in which God and his creatures reach out to each other, is the context of the Incarnation; there is no other way to understand its full significance. Although it was unthinkable to the Israelites that the transcendent God should actually become a part of the human scene by taking on human form, the unthinkable occurred in the mystery of the Incarnation. God became man in Jesus of Nazareth. In Jesus, he identified fully with humanity. John's statement in the first chapter of his Gospel is simple and definitive: "The Word became flesh and made his dwelling among us" (John 1:14). The Incarnation constitutes an unbreakable link between God and the human family.

The immediate result of the Incarnation, as it unfolded in the life, death, resurrection and exaltation of Jesus, was our redemption. Paul told the Galatians:

> ... But when the designated time had come, God sent forth his Son born of a woman, born under the law, to deliver from the law those who were subjected to it, so that we might receive our status as adopted sons. The proof that you are sons is the fact that God has sent forth into our hearts the spirit of his Son which cries out "Abba" ("Father!"). You are no longer a slave but a son! And the fact that you are a son makes you an heir, by God's design. (Galatians 4:4-7)

The Incarnation established a new relationship not only between us and God but also among us human beings. We adopted children of the Father are Christ's brothers and sisters and, in him, brothers and sisters of one another. Jesus made very clear the inseparability of love of God and love of neighbor: "This is the first" of all the commandments, he said:

> " 'Hear, O Israel! The Lord our God is Lord alone!
> Therefore you shall love the Lord your God
> with all your heart,
> with all your soul,
> with all your mind,
> and with all your strength.'
> This is the second,
> 'You shall love your neighbor as yourself.' "
>
> (Mark 12:29-31)

To follow Jesus one must love all those whom he loves. There is no other way.

It is of crucial importance that we understand and

appreciate the Incarnation's significance for the human condition in its many dimensions. That God redeemed us through the *humanity* of his Son has tremendous implications for how we understand ourselves and the meaning of our lives.

For example, the Incarnation rules out any kind of dualism which would radically separate the human body and soul. Such dualism sets body and soul in opposition as if they were essentially separate entities, with the soul considered to be what is properly human in a person, while the body is thought to be subhuman, inferior, of scant value. In such a view the body's role is limited to housing the soul for a short time, so that what happens to the body has little or no impact on one's real self.

The Incarnation rules out this view because to become truly human, the Word became *flesh*. (Hence, too, the necessary truth that Jesus rose *bodily* from the dead. Conquering death involved for him, as it will for us, not the attenuated existence of a disembodied spirit but true, resurrected bodily life.)

Thus, in redeeming us through his death and resurrection, Jesus redeemed the whole person, body and soul. Evidently, then, the Incarnation teaches us that bodiliness is an integral part of our own identity, as it was of the Word-become-flesh. It is not something "out there"—something removed from our personhood to be abused or manipulated without harm to our real selves. A human person is a bodily person. And this substantial unity of the material and the spiritual in the human person has important implications for the moral life, helping us to make ethical judgments about such "bodily" things as our sexuality and some current and future projects of biotechnology. To violate the integrity of the human body is to violate the integrity of the human person.

There is tremendous significance for the human family in Jesus' appearance among us and the continued presence of the risen Lord in the world. Above all, Jesus is the sign and cause of our redemption. Because he became flesh and redeemed us through his death and resurrection, we are now "new creations," as Paul told the Corinthians: "This means that if anyone is in Christ, he is a new creation. The old order has passed away; now all is new!" (2 Corinthians 5:17).

We are a people called to a new intimacy and friendship with God; a people with an eternal destiny, who even now have begun to experience the treasures of the heavenly Kingdom. We are a people who reflect, with new brightness and beauty, the image and likeness of God; a people who, in the totality of our humanity, are expected to express the values which Jesus realized in his own life. We are a people to whom much has been given and from whom much will be expected.

There can be no dichotomy between the material and the spiritual, between flesh and spirit, between the divine and the human. They are distinct, of course, but not opposed. In becoming man, Jesus brought into a new and higher harmony these diverse elements whose original harmony had been fractured by sin.

The only absolute dichotomy or division a fatal one, spiritually—is that between Jesus and the forces opposed to him. But as Jesus triumphed over sin and death, we also can overcome evil and death by being united with him in faith and love. We "overcome" evil, of course, precisely as he did—by redemptive suffering. The Cross is central to Christian life. That is because sin, both original and personal, and its consequences are still very much with us.

In sum, the Incarnation puts us and the kind of life we are expected to live in a totally new perspective. As Christians, we are fully human and also in a true sense, divine; for what we call "grace" is our participation in the divine life. To be fully and authentically human, therefore, means striving for the highest sanctity. One who sees this simply cannot be satisfied with being a mediocre or marginal Christian.

As a people redeemed by Jesus' blood, we are called to a radically new way of life in which the criteria of success are totally different from the world's criteria. Now that the Word has become flesh, we cannot be overly concerned with ourselves—our petty vanities and prejudices, our hostilities and fleeting attachments. We have a higher calling. To be sure, we see now as in a glass darkly; yet, seeing with the eyes of faith, we begin even now to discern the "new heavens and a new earth" (Revelation 21:1) which are to come fully into being through Christ's power at the end of time. Our vision must not be limited. We have work to do—our share in restoring all things in Christ. We must take off the blinders, so that we can see "the splendor of the gospel showing forth the glory of Christ, the image of God" (2 Corinthians 4:4).

## Jesus Is the Way, the Truth and the Life

Only through Jesus can we fully approach the Father and come to know him.

> "I am the way, and the truth, and the life;
> no one comes to the Father but through me." (John 14:6)

Impossible though it is to plumb the depths of this statement, its meaning for us is nevertheless clear enough: In and through Jesus we come to God.

*Jesus is the Way.* In what sense is Jesus our *way* to the Father? First, by his death and resurrection. Through the events we call the "Paschal Mystery" Jesus reconciled us with his Father. As Paul told the Romans, Jesus "was handed over to death for our sins and raised up for our justification" (Romans 4:25).

The Lord's death and resurrection are not just historical events which happened in a particular time and place; they are life-giving events whose power permeates our lives. Their impact will never cease. More than that, those who seek to follow Christ are called in a mysterious way to participate in these events and reenact them. Paul expressed this when he told the Corinthians:

> Continually we carry about in our bodies the dying of Jesus, so that in our bodies the life of Jesus may also be revealed. While we live we are constantly being delivered to death for Jesus' sake, so that the life of Jesus may be revealed in our mortal flesh. (2 Corinthians 4:10-11)

Our duty as Christians is to continue Jesus' redemptive mission in the world today.

Jesus is also our way to the Father through the Church which he established to continue his saving mission. He made it clear from the very beginning that his mission had a communitarian dimension. Certainly there was a deep personal relationship between him and each of the disciples, as there is between him and each of us today. But he was also related to them, and is related to us, as to a community united by faith in and commitment to him. The Gospels tell us how he formed this community, teaching and challenging its members, encouraging and even correcting them when necessary.

Before returning to his Father, Jesus took steps to ensure the continued stability of the community of his followers. Not even their fear and despondency during the terrible events of Good Friday robbed them of their identity and unity as believers in the Lord Jesus. After the resurrection, when the Holy Spirit came to them, they emerged as a courageous and determined group, ready and indeed eager to begin proclaiming Jesus and his gospel to a hostile world. The Acts of the Apostles tells us:

> The community of believers were of one heart and one mind. None of them ever claimed anything as his own; rather, everything was held in common. With power the apostles bore witness to the resurrection of the Lord Jesus, and great respect was paid to them all.
>
> (Acts 4:32-33)

They gave this witness by devoting themselves to "the apostles' instruction and the communal life, to the breaking of the bread and the prayers" (Acts 2:42). Acts, as well as the Epistles, also tell us of of the suffering and martyrdom which so many members of the early Christian communities willingly suffered for Jesus' sake.

Plainly, then, the Church is no mere organization; it is a community of faith over which the risen Lord presides and through which the baptized make their pilgrim way to the Father. Nor is the Church something optional, a kind of religious club to which one can belong or not, according to individual taste and temperament. The Church cannot be separated from Christ. Christian life, which is essentially communitarian, is to be lived in the community Christ founded. As I remarked before, it makes no sense to say, as some do, that one accepts Christ but rejects the Church.

Why, then, do people take this attitude? In some cases, I believe, because they wish to avoid the obligations which accepting Christ in his Church would entail. But others are sincere—they find it hard to see Christ in a community which in the past and also today has at times fallen tragically short of the high standards proclaimed by Christ.

The Church is not an impersonal institution; it is made

up of people. Jesus himself warned that there would always be wicked and insensitive people among us. Even those who were privileged to be in Jesus' immediate company during his life on earth often bickered among themselves, misunderstood his message, fell short of the standards he set for them. One betrayed him, and their chief, Peter, denied him.

Today, too, all of us can recognize failings in ourselves which dim Christ's image in the Church. The presence of weakness and evil in the Church—that is, in us who *are* the Church—is simply a reminder that we are all sinful and always in need of forgiveness and healing. But Jesus does not reject the Church because of our sinfulness. Rather, he acts continually

> ... to make her holy, purifying her in the bath of water by the power of the word, to present to himself a glorious church, holy and immaculate, without stain or wrinkle or anything of that sort. (Ephesians 5:26-27)

We must cooperate with him in this work, purifying the Church by purifying ourselves.

A clear pastoral imperative flows from all this. Not only have we been redeemed by Christ, we are to *continue* Christ's redemptive mission in the world, individually and together with the other members of Christ's Church. This requires striving to be absolutely faithful, as he was, to the Father's will and to overcome evil primarily through redemptive suffering.

*Jesus is the Truth.* Jesus is also the way to the Father because he reveals to us his Father's *truth.* But this Son does more than just tell us about his Father; he *is* the Father's revelation to us.

> In times past, God spoke in fragmentary and varied ways to our fathers through the prophets; in this, the final age, he has spoken to us through his Son, whom he has made heir of all things and through whom he first created the universe. This Son is the reflection of the Father's glory, the exact representation of the Father's being....
> (Hebrews 1:1-3)

First of all, Jesus reveals the Father to us in his very

being and life—that is, precisely in his humanity, which our senses can perceive and our minds can grasp. The opening words of the First Epistle of John declare this truth and convey the wonderment Christians have always felt in contemplating it:

> This is what we proclaim to you:
> what was from the beginning,
> what we have heard,
> what we have seen with our eyes,
> what we have looked upon
> and our hands have touched—
> we speak of the word of life.
> (This life became visible;
> we have seen and bear witness to it,
> and we proclaim to you the eternal life
> that was present to the Father
> and became visible to us.) (1 John 1:1-2)

Above all in his death and resurrection Jesus reveals to us his Father's great love and his plan for the human family.

> "There is no greater love than this:
> to lay down one's life for one's friends. . . .
> I no longer speak of you as slaves,
> for a slave does not know what his master is about.
> Instead, I call you friends,
> since I have made known to you all that I heard from my
>     Father." (John 15:13, 15)

Jesus also reveals his Father to us through his teaching. He constantly taught his followers about his Father and what he expected of them. As we know from the Gospels, he taught in a very simple, down-to-earth way, especially in parables. So compelling was his personality that people were eager to hear what he had to say, even though he called them to a way of life not always to their liking. His miracles testified to the credibility of his words. "They were spellbound by his teaching," Luke tells us, "for his words had authority" (Luke 4:32).

Jesus' teaching mission did not end with his public ministry. He promised to send the Holy Spirit, who would instruct us in everything and remind us of all Jesus had told us while he was on earth (cf. John 14:26). As Paul said,

> The Spirit we have received is not the world's spirit but God's Spirit, helping us to recognize the gifts he has given us. (1 Corinthians 2:12)

This teaching mission of Jesus is carried on through his Spirit *in the Church.* Jesus promised the Church special assistance so that his followers would never have to be in serious doubt or error concerning the essential elements of his teaching.

Learning more about the truth Jesus has revealed to us and growing in fidelity to that truth are essential to our relationship with him. That relationship is of questionable authenticity if we have little regard for what he has revealed to us—if we do not feel obligated to seek the truth and shape our lives by it. Furthermore, his doctrine is essentially self-revelation: Not to believe what he teaches is not to believe in him. Hence the importance of the Church's teaching mission and our duty to be faithful to what the Church teaches in his name.

Pope John Paul II emphasized the importance of truth when he spoke to the Mexican bishops in 1979 about their teaching role:

> As pastors, you have the vivid awareness that your principal duty is to be teachers of the truth. Not a human and rational truth, but the truth that comes from God, the truth that brings with it the authentic liberation of man: "you will know the truth, and the truth will make you free" (John 8:32).[4]

He then spoke about the truth concerning Jesus, the Church and its mission, and ourselves. Only if we know the truth about all three can we have a correct understanding of what we are about today, together with a clear vision of our destiny and the means of attaining it.

*Jesus is the Life.* Finally, Jesus is our way to the Father because in and through him we are restored to grace and grow in supernatural *life*. In and through Jesus we are "reborn" in the spiritual order—we become a new creation:

> ... you must lay aside your former way of life and the old self which deteriorates through illusion and desire, and acquire a fresh, spiritual way of thinking. You must put on that new man created in God's image, whose justice and holiness are born of truth. (Ephesians 4:22-24)

Jesus—and only he—is the source of spiritual regeneration.

Jesus breathes his divine life of grace into us through the sacraments. Yet today, even within the Church, some tend to downplay their importance. Why not encounter Jesus directly, they ask, instead of approaching him through sacraments? This sadly misses the point.

For one thing, Jesus instituted the sacraments for our benefit. He expects one who knows this and has access to the sacraments to take advantage of them. A person who accepts Jesus but at the same time rejects his precious gifts is not acting consistently.

The crucial thing about these gifts of the Lord is that, far from being alternatives to a direct encounter with Christ, they *are* our life-giving means of encountering him. It is Jesus who cleanses us and welcomes us into his Church in Baptism. Similarly, it is Jesus who strengthens us in our apostolate in Confirmation, Jesus who forgives our sins in Penance—Jesus who is present and active in each of these seven signs of his great love for us.

To grasp fully the significance of the sacraments it is necessary to see them from an incarnational perspective. Jesus redeemed us in a very *human* way. He became man; he suffered and died for us; after he rose from the dead, his disciples saw him and ate and talked with him—indeed, he even invited Thomas to place his hand in the wounds of the crucifixion in order to dispel his lingering doubts about the reality of what had happened on Easter Sunday.

Jesus has chosen, for our sakes, to remain present and active among us in a way equally suited to our human, bodily condition. Knowing how eager we are to see and tangibly experience whatever most affects our well-being, he gave us the sacraments, which are both signs and occasions of his saving presence and grace. In the sacraments, constituted by simple elements and familiar words, we truly encounter the Lord who shares with us his divine life and prepares us for the important moments of this life as well as the next. In celebrating the sacraments we experience a foretaste of the peace and joy of his kingdom which will be ours in their fullness when we are united with him in the next world.

# Chapter 2

# Our Response in Faith to Jesus

**H**aving spoken of who Jesus is and of the significance of his presence in the world, I wish now to reflect more deeply on the personal response which he expects of us. And it must be a *personal* response. For we profess faith in a person, Jesus Christ, Son of Man and Lord of all creation. St. Paul says of him:

> Though he was in the form of God,
>> he did not deem equality with God
>> something to be grasped at.

> Rather, he emptied himself
>> and took the form of a slave,
>> being born in the likeness of men.

> He was known to be of human estate,
>> and it was thus that he humbled himself,
>> obediently accepting even death,
>> death on a cross!

> Because of this,
>> God highly exalted him
>> and bestowed on him the name
>> above every other name,

> So that at Jesus' name
>> every knee must bend
>> in the heavens, on the earth,
>> and under the earth,
>> and every tongue proclaim

to the glory of God the Father:
JESUS CHRIST IS LORD! (Philippians 2:6-11)

This Jesus is not a myth, an abstraction or a mere memory. He is alive and close to us—now, at this very moment. He is brother, he is lover, he is friend. He cares about us, about our well-being and needs, about our joys and sorrows. Like all those who love us, he expresses his love through concern and service and support.

But he also has more to give than the rest of our friends. He invites us to share, through the mystery we call grace, his own life—that unending, vibrant, glorified life he received from the Father. As St. John tells us:

Yes, God so loved the world
that he gave his only Son,
that whoever believes in him may not die
but may have eternal life. (John 3:16)

Faith, then, is our response to the person of Jesus; it is a personal and individual response to his personal presence in us and in our world. Certainly faith has an intellectual content, truths we must hold and profess because they are part of God's self-revelation in Jesus. But in the end, to use the words of Thomas More in *A Man for All Seasons,* "It isn't a matter of reason.... Finally, it's a matter of love."[5] The only fitting response to love is love.

Unfortunately, some people feel that they attend adequately to their spiritual lives by participating in religious exercises in a more or less unreflective and perfunctory way. They have no sense of being personally challenged to surrender themselves completely to Jesus.

But unless we see at the center of Christianity a personal relationship with God through Christ and in the Holy Spirit, we risk reducing our religion to a philosophy of life, a set of principles, a code of conduct—all of which we can master and manipulate. Christianity does involve those things, but it is also infinitely more. Essentially, it is a personal, loving relationship with a living person, Jesus Christ.

For this relationship to flourish and deepen, we must be open, attentive and ready to grow. I am so convinced of this personal dimension of Christianity that in 1977, in my last address as president to the National Conference of Catholic Bishops, I stated:

> The most important task of a bishop—and the supreme reason for which his leadership is sought in the Church—is to proclaim Christ Jesus and his Good News in such a way as to elicit a deep, personal commitment to him and acceptance of his message. Like St. Paul, "We must preach not ourselves, but Jesus Christ as Lord.... For God who commanded light to shine out of darkness, has shone in our hearts to give enlightenment concerning the knowledge of the glory of God, shining on the face of Jesus Christ" (2 Cor. 4:5-6). This is the work of evangelization, which aims at conversion.[6]

I went on to explain how, as bishops, we should be evangelizers. I also pointed out that proclaiming Christ and his gospel is a responsibility of the entire Church, not just the bishops.

This talk elicited a greater response, from all parts of the country, than any other I gave as president of the bishops' conference. Why? Surely the Church has always known that its primary responsibility is to preach the Lord Jesus, to continue his saving presence in the world so that people will come to know and love him and enter into intimate relationships with him.

One reason for the extraordinary response, I believe, is this: We are emerging from the first, immediate phase of the intense renewal of the Church called for by Vatican Council II. During these years much time was spent developing new structures and new ways of doing things, so that the Church would be in a position to fulfill its mission more effectively. With this work nearing completion, many people now perceive more keenly than before that renewal's basic purpose is not structural change but better, more zealous proclamation of the Lord and his gospel. And that requires changing much more than structures; it requires changing minds and hearts.

I believe there is also another reason why the talk attracted attention. Our world is dominated by secular and material values. God is simply not the most important person in many people's lives. As a result, more and more people experience apathy and indifference, alienation and hostility toward the Church, even to the point of no longer practicing their religion and falling away from the faith.

At the same time, those who remain committed to the Church are more aware than ever of the need to make the Lord known to those who have turned away from him. They desire to show in a concrete and credible way that the Christian faith is as relevant as it ever was—that, without faith in the Lord, even the greatest of human accomplishments have little lasting value. And these committed Catholics realize that, as things now stand in the Church and the world, they cannot sit back and do nothing. While the grace of conversion and faith comes from God, *we* are the human instruments he uses to draw people to himself. Jesus' mandate to the apostles is meant for us, too: "Go into the whole world and proclaim the good news to all creation" (Mark 16:15).

Our most urgent need, as individuals and as a community of believers, is total commitment to the Lord and all he has taught us. We must put him first in our lives and give priority over everything else to his message of salvation, as handed on by the Church. To do this we must abandon ourselves completely to him, placing ourselves in his hands and letting him make us instruments of his saving presence in the world. To put it simply, we must let go, so that there will be no obstacle in our lives separating us from the Lord.

This turning to Jesus is conversion. Initial conversion may be a sudden event, but thoroughgoing conversion— sanctity—is the work of a lifetime, a work to which we all are called. John the Baptist, who prepared the way for the appearance of Jesus, cried out to the people of his day: "Reform your lives! The reign of God is at hand" (Matthew 3:2). St. Paul, after Jesus' appearance, told the Corinthians: "We implore you, in Christ's name: be reconciled to God!" (2 Corinthians 5:20). That call to conversion is as valid today as it ever was. "If we say, 'We are free of the guilt of sin,' we deceive ourselves; the truth is not to be found in us" (1 John 1:8). No matter who we are, no matter how much we think of ourselves, no matter how much God may have blessed us—we are sinners. We need conversion.

Conversion means turning away from the evil in our

lives and more and more making our own the mind and heart of Jesus. It means transforming our lives into his so that he can live in us. Paul said it best, I think: "... the life I live now is not my own; Christ is living in me" (Galatians 2:20).

Few, if any, of us are Christians of Paul's stature, but a real personal relationship with Jesus is nevertheless possible for us as it was for Paul. Jesus wants us to have such a relationship, and he can and will bring it about if we cooperate with him.

Such a relationship with Jesus is not reserved for mystics, nor is it exclusively the result of a highly emotional "experience" of Christ. It is true that in many cases the experience of conversion does seem to be very intense and emotional; but, even so, that ordinarily passes in time, and one is left with the everyday challenge—a welcome one—of maintaining and deepening the relationship which began with the conversion experience. This is not unlike the familiar process where, having met a person by whom one is deeply impressed, one goes about taking the continuing and often not very exciting steps required to build up and enrich the relationship over a period of time.

How then are we to establish, maintain and deepen a personal relationship with Jesus? There are two basic and indispensable ways: prayer and participation in the sacramental life of the Church. Union with the Lord through personal and liturgical prayer and the sacraments in turn releases within us a great force, which shapes not only our own spiritual growth but our relationships with others. Let us see more closely what this means.

Chapter 3

# The Following
# of Christ

**W**e saw earlier that the sacraments are encounters with Jesus. Now let us probe more deeply how union with the Lord is strengthened and enriched through participation in the sacramental life of the Church. Then we shall consider prayer, for it, too, is essential to establishing and maintaining a relationship with God. Finally, I hope to show how prayer and the sacraments shape our behavior as Christians in the world.

### The Eucharist and Penance

I shall focus here on the Eucharist and Penance. These are the sacraments we celebrate regularly throughout life. How we use them makes a great difference, for better or worse, in how we relate to the Lord and also to one another.

*Our encounter with Jesus in the Eucharist.* Jesus is truly present—body, blood, soul and divinity—in the Eucharist, under the appearances of bread and wine. We cannot fathom this great mystery of faith, but the Church has always taken quite literally what Jesus said at the Last Supper:

> During the meal Jesus took bread, blessed it, broke it, and gave it to his disciples. "Take this and eat it," he said, "this is my body." Then he took a cup, gave thanks, and gave it to them. "All of you must drink from it," he said, "for this is my blood, the blood of the covenant, to be poured out in behalf of many for the forgiveness of sins."
> (Matthew 26:26-28)

27

Earlier in his ministry Jesus had intimated to his disciples that he would give himself to them in the Eucharist. The miracle of the multiplication of the loaves and fish, recounted by all four evangelists, has traditionally been considered a sign not only of Jesus' power as God's Son and his compassion for the hungry people who had followed him, but also as a foreshadowing of something far greater—the Eucharist. Through the Eucharist, Jesus' redemptive act is continued through time in a way that makes it possible for us to participate in it.

The Eucharist is a dynamic reality. Jesus' presence in the Eucharist is active, not passive, capable of making a tremendous impact on our lives as individuals and as a community of believers.

A meal was an important occasion for the people of biblical times, as it is for us. In the Old Testament, the Passover, one of the most sacred events for the Jewish people, was celebrated each year by a religious rite which took the specific form of a family meal. This is natural: A meal shared with family or friends is a sign of human intimacy. To invite a person to one's table is a mark of trust, confidence and affection; to accept the invitation is to return these sentiments. Thus a meal shared in a religious context, such as the Passover meal, is a sign of the intimacy among the participants as well as their intimacy with God.

It was at a meal, the Last Supper, that Jesus gave his disciples his greatest gift—himself. In doing so, he expressed his great love for them and also for us. As part of his total redemptive act, completed on the cross the next day, the Last Supper had a sacrificial character: It was a forceful sign of his gift of self for our salvation. Moreover, by commanding the apostles and those who came after them to continue to celebrate this sacred meal until the end of time and by promising that whenever that was done he would be truly present under the appearances of bread and wine, Jesus perpetuated his saving presence among us, while also making the celebration of the Eucharist not only his action but the Church's.

The Eucharist both memorializes and truly reenacts the great mystery which is central to our salvation: Jesus' sacrificial death on the cross and his resurrection. Now, however, we share in Christ's action. Celebrating the Eucharist in union with Jesus, we worship the Father, giving him thanks for all he has done for us. We join in Jesus' offering and offer our lives in union with his. In this sacred meal we receive Jesus, the Bread of Life, who nourishes and sustains us spiritually. The Eucharist is moreover a sign of and an initial participation in the heavenly banquet where we will be in total communion with God—Father, Son and Holy Spirit.

Thus, we believe as Catholics that the Mass is at the same time and inseparably

> , , , a sacrifice in which the Sacrifice of the Cross is perpetuated; a memorial of the death and resurrection of the Lord... ; [and] a sacred banquet in which, through the communion of the body and blood of the Lord, the people of God share the benefits of the paschal sacrifice, renew the new Covenant which God has made with the human family once for all through the blood of Christ, and in faith and hope foreshadow and anticipate ... the banquet in the Kingdom of the Father, proclaiming the Lord's death "till his coming."[7]

The Eucharist has still another dimension. No one can partake sincerely of the sacred banquet while remaining indifferent to his brothers and sisters. The Eucharist unites us in the love of Christ, and this is a love to be shared with others, a love that commits us to their devoted service.

In this way the Eucharist, properly understood and celebrated, is a source of social consciousness and of moral imperatives for the life of the Church as a whole and for each of its members individually. Not a purely private action, affecting only the individuals who directly participate in it, the Mass is instead a celebration of the entire Church, calling the faith community to foster the well-being of the human family by bringing Jesus' love, mercy, justice and compassion to bear upon its earthy pilgrimage. The Second Vatican Council expressed this with succinct eloquence in calling the Eucharist "a meal of brotherly solidarity."[8]

No wonder, then, that the Mass is at the very heart of Catholic life and worship! Nothing else so well expresses what we believe and are as baptized Christians, completely dedicated to the Lord. In celebrating the Eucharist, the Church experiences the presence of its risen Lord in a unique way and unites itself with him in his saving action. Truly the sacred liturgy, especially the Eucharistic Sacrifice, as the Council told us, is the source and summit of the Church's worship, mission and life.[9]

For one who grasps this, participation in the Eucharistic Liturgy is no mere external ritual but an experience intimately related to conversion to the Lord and life with him. But let us be honest. We know that it is possible—even easy—for our participation in the Eucharist to be slack and indifferent.

This is so when, unresponsive to God's grace, we raise barriers to Jesus and refuse to reflect in our lives his goodness and truth, his love and mercy, his justice, his understanding and compassion. As Paul told the Philippians, our thoughts and our actions must always be "directed to all that is true, all that deserves respect, all that is honest, pure, admirable, decent, virtuous, or worthy of praise" (Philippians 4:8). If it is otherwise with us, we may "go to Mass" but we remain unchanged.

Sometimes people say they have stopped going to Mass because they get little out of it; the Mass is not a "meaningful experience." Often they blame the Church and its liturgy. True, poorly planned and poorly celebrated liturgies can present obstacles. But in some cases the real obstacle lies elsewhere. Not failures by the Church and its representatives, but individual failure to live by gospel values may lie at the heart of the problem. Those whose lives are not faith-filled and whose priorities are not gospel-oriented will hardly be able to see and experience the Lord in the sacred rites.

One of my favorite Gospel stories tells of the encounter of the risen Jesus with the two disciples on the road to Emmaus (cf. Luke 24: 13-35). We all know it well. Traveling from Jerusalem, the disciples were reviewing the recent events. A stranger approached and asked them what they were talking about so animatedly. Their answer was slightly condescending: "Are you the only resident of Jerusalem who does not know the things that went on there these past few days?" The stranger simply asked, "What things?"

The two men then related all that had happened to their friend Jesus. They began with his trial, told of his crucifixion and death, and concluded with the report of the empty tomb. They seemed not to have been altogether persuaded on the latter point. Yes, witnesses had returned from the tomb saying they had seen angels there who told them Jesus was alive. And the tomb was certainly empty. But where was Jesus himself? Their keen disappointment was evident when they added, "We were hoping that he was the one who would set Israel free."

The stranger's response was surprising—and impatient. "What little sense you have! How slow you are to believe all that the prophets have announced! Did not the Messiah have to undergo all this so as to enter into his glory?" Then—now very patiently, as Luke tell us—"beginning ... with Moses and all the prophets, he interpreted for them every passage of Scripture which referred to him."

By the time they reached Emmaus, the two disciples were so fascinated with the stranger that they begged him to stay and have supper with them. He agreed. Luke tells us that "when he had seated himself with them to eat, he took bread, pronounced the blessing, then broke the bread and began to distribute it to them. With that their eyes were opened and they recognized him; whereupon he vanished from their sight."

In an instant the two disciples changed radically. They came alive. "Were not our hearts burning inside us as he talked to us on the road and explained the Scriptures to us?" Hurrying back to Jerusalem, they enthusiastically told the apostles and all the others who were with them: "The Lord has been raised! It is true!" Never again would they doubt. Their beloved Jesus was alive. All their time and energy would go to proclaiming the risen Christ to the world. The work of evangelization had begun.

Whenever we celebrate the Eucharist, Jesus speaks to us in the Scriptures and he "breaks bread" and shares it with us. Do we see him with the eyes of faith? Do we recognize him and welcome him into our lives, so that, loving us, he can share with us the graces of redemption? The two disciples were slow to recognize him, but at last they did—in the breaking of the bread. Do we? Or do we fail even then to grasp his presence among us? While hearing his words and participating in the breaking of the bread, do we yet remain unchanged by Jesus' saving power because we do not wish to change? Does pride or an attachment to someone or something stand between us and the Lord, blinding us to his presence and preventing us from responding to his love?

May we open our hearts wide to Jesus in the Eucharist. May we not be afraid or hold back. In the powerlessness of the crucified Jesus we find our power as a redeemed people. In the triumph of the risen Christ we find our life and glory.

*Our encounter with Jesus' forgiving and healing power.* On the evening of the day that Jesus rose from the dead, the apostles gathered fearfully behind locked doors. Suddenly Jesus was with them. After bestowing his peace upon them and, just as the Father had sent him, sending them forth to continue his work, he breathed on them and said:

> "Receive the Holy Spirit.
> If you forgive men's sins,
> they are forgiven them;
> if you hold them bound,
> they are held bound." (John 20:22-23)

These words refer very directly to the sacramental ministry of reconciliation—that is, to Penance.

Today this sacrament is in eclipse for many. Not that Penance has lost its wonderful power, but fewer people feel the need for it. Any parish priest can confirm that the number of confessions has radically decreased in recent years.

This is unfortunate, even tragic. The need for reconciliation is as great now as it ever was. Perhaps the "sense of sin" has dimmed for many, but despite exaggerated statements one sometimes hears about the near impossibility of committing sin, deep down most of us know better. We know we are weak and sinful, and Scripture testifies to this.

> If we say, "We are free of the guilt of sin,"
> we deceive ourselves; the truth is not to be found in us.
> But if we acknowledge our sins,
> he who is just can be trusted
> to forgive our sins
> and cleanse us from every wrong.
> If we say, "We have never sinned,"

we make him a liar
and his word finds no place in us. (1 John 1:8-10)

Aware of our sinfulness, we instinctively feel the need
to be forgiven. We crave to open up to someone, admit our
shortcomings and then be told that we are loved and pardoned.
Above all, we crave to hear this from the Lord. And that is what
the Sacrament of Penance or Reconciliation is all about. Here
we encounter the Lord Jesus and experience his forgiving,
healing love.

The new rite of Penance encourages us to avoid a rote
and unreflective use of the sacrament. Penance is much more
than a mechanical recitation of sins. We must tell our faults,
fully and honestly, but in doing so we should also probe more
deeply, seeking the sinful attitudes and habits that underlie our
sinful deeds and striving to uproot them. The Lord stands ready
to help. Jesus offers himself to us not as a condemning judge
but as a redeeming savior, eager to embrace us with his love
and healing if only we ask.

Furthermore, by providing for communal Penance
services, the new rite helps us experience the social dimension
of both our sinfulness and our forgiveness in the Church. Sin
disrupts our relationship both with God and with our brothers
and sisters. This point is crucial to grasping the connection
between personal sin and the disorders and injustices of society.

Today, too, the sacrament's link with Baptism and the
Eucharist needs to be brought into clearer focus, while the
integral relationship between repentance, penitential practices
and an authentic Christian life also is emphasized.
Relationships broken by sin must be restored; the Sacrament of
Penance is therefore a necessary element of spiritual growth.
We must approach the sacrament humbly and sincerely,
acknowledging that we are sinners who, needing God's
forgiveness, wish to repent, to change, to be converted. Perhaps
most of all, we must have deep confidence in God's love, in his
willingness to forgive and his power to heal and change us.

It would be a mistake to think of Penance only as a
kind of emergency remedy, a way of obtaining pardon for
serious sins and no more than that. This sacrament is
indispensable for *anyone* striving to make progress in the
spiritual life. Its frequent reception can make a world of

difference in how we relate to God, to others and even to ourselves.

That has surely been my experience. The Sacrament of Penance is an essential part of my spiritual life. As time passes, this becomes more and more clear to me. How alone, discouraged and even helpless I would feel at times if I did not approach Jesus in this sacrament; if I did not tell him of my personal faults and weaknesses along with my concerns, my hopes, my aspirations; if I did not receive from Jesus, through the priest-confessor, assurance of his forgiveness and his love—assurance that, if I try to do my part, he will always be at my side to help me. Approached in this spirit, Penance provides a rich experience of Jesus' love and mercy and serves as a source of true joy and consolation.

## The Role of Prayer in Christian Life

Like the Eucharist and Penance, prayer also brings us into closer union with Jesus. In doing so, it helps us know ourselves better and relate more lovingly and intimately to others. In each of these aspects it can transform us.

Today there is much evidence of renewed interest in spirituality and prayer. Despite material and secular pressures, people are praying. Here we have a reaffirmation of a tradition that goes back to the beginnings of faith.

Jesus was a man of prayer. The Gospels tell us he prayed before all the important events in his life. Before beginning his public ministry, he went into the desert to fast and pray for 40 days. And what intense prayer he experienced in the garden of Gethsemane the night before making the supreme gift of himself to his Father on our behalf! Similarly, St. Paul speaks often in his letters of his own need for prayer and the need of those to whom he writes. "Never cease praying," he tells the Thessalonians, "render constant thanks; such is God's will for you in Christ Jesus" (1 Thessalonians 5:17-18).

Christ's followers must be people of prayer. But it is important to know what prayer involves. What kind of prayer were Jesus and the apostles talking about? What should be prayer's effect on us?

The answers which follow, flowing from my own spiritual journey, are meant to be of help and encouragement to you in yours. I may not be able to shed much light on the dark areas you have encountered, but perhaps just knowing that you are not alone will encourage you to persevere.

These reflections, which specifically concern personal prayer, take for granted the centrality in Christian life of communal, liturgical prayer. Personal prayer and liturgical prayer are not competitors; they complement each other. Personal prayer is, among other things, a way of preparing for liturgical prayer, while liturgical prayer is, among other things, a source of inspiration and nourishment for personal prayer.

If I speak here mainly of personal prayer, that is because of the growing interest in the subject which I noted above, and because, alongside the interest, many people have genuine questions, even doubts, about their ability to undertake and continue this admittedly difficult but enormously important spiritual practice.

*Prayer as discovery of self.* Prayer can change our lives. Authentic prayer does not insulate us from the real world, nor is it a crutch on which to lean in order to avoid facing up realistically to life. Rather, prayer which brings us into intimate, loving union with God influences, deeply and for the better, how we perceive and deal with others and with ourselves.

To pray effectively requires practice, engagement and regularity—the constant doing of it. Even someone whose faith is weak or sporadic can pray in a crisis; but as good as that may be it is much better that prayer be a regular, continuing part of our lives. Love can hardly grow and flourish without communication. And prayer is the dialogue of human and divine lovers. Thus the saints of every age have insisted, as Christ did, on the need to "pray constantly" so that the heart may know its beloved and the Lord may become as present to us as our very breathing.

But considering the typically overextended schedules which most of us struggle to maintain, how can we pray—and constantly—in season and out, when convenient and inconvenient? Too often we pray only when we feel like it and find it convenient. That is a formula for praying seldom. We must find time for prayer not in the rare lulls in our schedules, but despite our "busy-ness," alongside it, in its very midst.

No matter how little or how much we have, we will be moved to pray if we are truly in love with Jesus and yearn to be with him; if we long to hear him speak what we most need to hear: "Repent and believe the Good News.... Follow me.... Come aside and pray with me awhile.... As I have done, so also must you do to your brothers.... I am with you...."

The absolute necessity of making time for prayer came home to me very forcefully a few years ago. My schedule was unbelievable. For several days in a row I was sure I simply did not have time to do more than celebrate Mass and pray a small part of the Liturgy of the Hours. Suddenly it dawned on me: "My life for many years to come will probably be as busy as it has been the past several days. Therefore, never again will I have the time to pray as I should." Immediately I saw the absurdity of the situation and determined to make prayer a real priority in my life. Doing so has required constant discipline but, happily, it has made a great difference in my life.

Spiritual writers tell us there are many kinds of prayer. All can be described as conversation or dialogue with God which begins in hearing, accepting and responding to his revelation. But this "conversation" can and does take various forms. The four classical forms of prayer are vocal (that is, prayer expressed in words, either a fixed formula or one's own words), meditative, affective and contemplative. The terms are somewhat strange and ponderous, but the experience to which they refer is direct and simple—as direct and simple as any exchange between two persons who love each other.

Today many people are rediscovering and using an ancient method called "centering prayer." This is really a form of contemplative prayer. One of its advantages is its simplicity, for the techniques involved make it accessible to everyone.

Centering prayer does not require keeping up a constant flow of words. Rather, with mind and heart open to any insight or manifestation of love the Lord may care to send, one simply acknowledges his presence and quietly enjoys it. Some call this "wasting time" with God, but the time is wasted only by worldly standards, which measure an investment of time by its tangible payoffs and rewards. In reality, this wasting of time in prayer nourishes and celebrates love. It demands "time out," timelessness, patience with one's whole life, patience to be with God.

Whatever method we use and however well or badly we use it, prayer, if it is genuine, must move us to a greater knowledge of ourselves. St. Teresa of Avila holds that one cannot grow closer to God without constantly growing in self-knowledge. Precisely for this reason, real growth in prayer involves a movement toward greater simplicity, that is, fewer words and thoughts. Both St. John of the Cross and Teresa say our own words and thoughts may lead us in the wrong direction; they may distract us from what God wants to show us about ourselves.

I hasten to add that prayer is not simply a process of introspection and self-analysis. Yet God cannot help us if we are unwilling to present ourselves to him as we are. Much of our time is spent pretending, trying to persuade others and even ourselves that we are someone other than we truly are. When we turn to God in prayer, however, we must present our real selves, candidly acknowledging our strengths and weaknesses and our total dependence on him. We should not be afraid to tell him all about our failings, our infidelities, our sins. To experience true conversion, we must first honestly face our innermost self which exists independently of external circumstances and pressures.

Let us consider some practical implications of self-knowledge. To know the truth about oneself in prayer includes honestly knowing one's motives. What do I want out of life? Why do I choose and act as I do? What guides me in my relationships with others? How important to me are acceptance and recognition? What roles do competition, fear, insecurity and resentment play in my life? Honest self-examination may lead us to conclude that, although our motives are not all "bad," they are frequently quite imperfect and, as such, can lead away from Jesus and his way of life.

In his letter to the Galatians, Paul describes forms of conduct arising from motivations which are of the Spirit, along with conduct arising from inclinations which are not. His description gives a good yardstick—that of external behavior—for judging our inner selves. It leaves no room for the notion that one can habitually do evil deeds yet be a good person at heart:

> It is obvious what proceeds from the flesh: lewd conduct, impurity, licentiousness, idolatry, sorcery, hostilities, bickering, jealousy, outbursts of rage, selfish rivalries,

dissensions, factions, envy, drunkenness, orgies, and the like.... In contrast, the fruit of the spirit is love, joy, peace, patient endurance, kindness, generosity, faith, mildness and chastity.... Since we live by the spirit, let us follow the spirit's lead. Let us never be boastful, or challenging, or jealous toward one another.

(Galatians 5:19-23, 25-26)

As we draw closer to God, that within us which is not of God is increasingly disclosed. But if we close our eyes to motivations or movements within us which are not of God, if we refuse to recognize the evil in us, that refusal itself becomes an obstacle to closer union with the Lord.

Often, of course, we are not fully conscious of what motivates us. We easily fool ourselves. That is why we need a spiritual director who, along with other vital, positive assistance rendered to us on our spiritual journey, can help us make objectively correct judgments about what is going on inside us.

Discovering our true selves can be a very painful experience. When we confront our ugly side, we tend at first to rebel. That is to be expected. But the suffering entailed in humbly acknowledging our own weakness and imperfection can itself be redemptive. We have been told to expect the cross in our lives, and sometimes the cross comes not from outside but from within. Did not Jesus say: "If a man wishes to come after me, he must deny his very self, take up his cross, and begin to follow in my footsteps" (Matthew 16:24)? The Letter to the Colossians goes further, saying that our suffering completes the process of purification required for our redemption: "In my own flesh I fill up what is lacking in the sufferings of Christ for the sake of his body, the church" (1:24).

Emotional satisfaction in prayer is not the necessary and exclusive sign that God loves us and is pleased with us. On the contrary, spiritual writers tell us that even for those who have committed themselves to prayer, the prevailing experience over long periods of time is not satisfaction but "dryness." In part this is our human reaction against the discipline of prayer; in part—and more significantly—it is God's way of teaching us to rely entirely on him.

That certainly has been my experience. I remember

once complaining to my spiritual director about the dryness troubling me. He asked how often I experienced spiritual satisfaction in prayer. Without giving it much thought, I said about half the time, perhaps a bit more. He smiled and told me that, if so, I was quite advanced spiritually; most people, even those very committed to prayer, experience satisfaction in praying far, far less often than that! I realized, of course, that I had exaggerated. The point is that we are being spiritually selfish in supposing that because we have put in our "time," we have a right to expect a "return" in the form of satisfaction. Authentic prayer is concerned not so much with getting as with giving.

Despite the dryness, however, if we are people of faith and fidelity, we will feel a certain restlessness or hunger calling us to communion with the Lord in prayer. For God never abandons us—he is always present, calling us to him. And hunger for communion with the Lord in the midst of dryness is actually the *gift* by which God calls us to himself.

This gift implants in us the desire to grow spiritually, to abandon ourselves completely to the Lord, to risk encountering him in prayer. And "risk" it is, for a true encounter with God in prayer may well provoke a crisis in our lives. His demands can be overwhelming—embarrassing, even devastating, in human terms. We may find ourselves called to make a radical, painful response. We secretly fear that if we hold back nothing and do just what the Lord wants of us, we will stop being the charming, witty people we are (or think we are) and turn into really odd people—as though God might cast an evil spell on us! And all the while God calls us to trust enough in his love and his power to risk knowing ourselves and encountering him.

*Prayer as discovery of others.* As I have said, however, self-discovery in prayer is not a sort of self-regarding spiritual narcissism. Why, after all, do we wish to know ourselves better in this way? First, as I have suggested, in order to present ourselves more honestly and openly to the Lord. But also in order to recognize more clearly our obligations to others—family, friends, neighbors, fellow workers—all those with whom we live and work and come in contact in the course of our lives.

To say this is to say that the goal of self-discovery in

prayer is a clearer grasp of and stronger commitment to one's personal vocation. What does God ask of me in the unique circumstances of my life? What practical implications does this have for my relationship with him and my efforts to serve my brothers and sisters in the Lord? Exploring personal vocation in the context of prayer necessarily involves a movement toward greater intimacy with others: with God first, of course, but also and in a particular way with other men and women.

The testimony of Scripture supports this view. Jesus made it very clear that love of God cannot be separated from love of neighbor.

The Incarnation adds a new and special dimension to this inseparable link between love of God and love of neighbor. The Father so loved us that he sent his Son to redeem us. Jesus became flesh and lived among us. So close and intimate a relationship does the Incarnation establish between us and God, and also among us human beings, that we can now call ourselves sons and daughters of the Father and brothers and sisters of and in the Lord. To follow the Lord, we must love all those whom he loves. There is no other way.

That is why, for example, racism so fundamentally contradicts our Christian faith. Racism rests on a denial of the essential equality of all human beings, based on our relationship to God as Creator and to Jesus Christ as Redeemer One who refuses to accept the fundamental unity of the human race in its origin and destiny rejects, knowingly or unknowingly the truth that God created us all and Christ died for us all. Racism is thus an attack on Christianity at its roots. So is any other attitude or behavior whose basic thrust toward others is discriminatory or exclusive. This is not the way of Jesus and the community of friendship with God which he founded.

Though we may often experience tension between love of God and love of others, we know that ultimately the two things cannot be separated. In his great parable of the Last Judgment Jesus makes this unmistakably clear:

> "Then the just will ask him: 'Lord, when did we see you hungry and feed you or see you thirsty and give you drink? When did we welcome you away from home or clothe you in your nakedness? When did we visit you when you were ill or in prison?' The king will answer

them: 'I assure you, as often as you did it for one of my
least brothers, you did it for me.' " (Matthew 25:37-40)

*The implications of Christian intimacy.* Our faith and everything
that flows from it—including our prayer—must be understood
in its incarnational perspective. That includes not only our new
relationship to God as redeemed people but also our new
relationship to all of God's children. Part of this relationship is
the God-given capacity to love others.

Any consideration of love inevitably touches the area of
sexuality. Unfortunately, many people understand sexuality in
too limited a way, identifying it almost exclusively with sexual
intercourse. While that is certainly a dimension of it, sexuality
is a much broader concept. Human sexuality is part of our
God-given natural power or capacity for relating to others in a
loving, caring way. From it flow the qualities of sensitivity,
warmth, openness and mutual respect in interpersonal
relationships.

If God's love lives in us and we nurture it by prayer, it
will be manifest in our ability to love others, to be present to
them in a caring way. The intimacy of which I speak is not
primarily genital, although love obviously can and should be
expressed in this way by two persons joined in the covenant of
marriage. Rather, for all people, married or single, this intimacy
means at least two things.

First, it means willingness to disclose oneself to others,
to become somewhat vulnerable with them by being honest
about oneself. That is hard for many of us. We think we look
weak when we reveal our weaknesses or needs—and pride or
fear blocks our self-revelation. So we hold things inside while
pressures build within us until, in some cases, we can no
longer cope successfully with them.

In the Sacrament of Penance the Lord has given us a
wonderful way of dealing with such pressures. Even humanly
speaking, people need opportunities to open up, to get things
out of their system. They need a way to be honest about their
inner self—including the evil within—and then to hear the
words, "I forgive you." I am not suggesting that the sacrament
is primarily a form of therapy; its operation and benefits are
essentially spiritual. But that in no way excludes the natural
benefits which it also confers.

Admittedly, the forum of the confessional is special—both sacred and limited. Generally speaking, we do not reveal ourselves even to close friends as we do to our confessor, and that is as it should be. But many matters outside the realm of the confessional cause us confusion, anxiety, depression and other negative feelings. Such matters can and should be shared with those who are close to us. More often than not, we will find that our friends experience the same difficulties. That discovery itself deepens the mutually beneficial bond of solidarity and understanding.

Second, intimacy involves willingness to let others become a part of and an influence on my life even as I become part of theirs. This is an important element of commitment and fidelity. Not only do I accept responsibility for those whom I love, care for and try to help—I strengthen the bonds of responsibility by allowing them to love me, care for me and help me in return. My life and my decisions are no longer simply my own; having let others into my life, I cannot fail to take them into consideration.

Precisely this willingness to assume responsibility for others is often missing in our world today. We have all heard accounts of people who were injured, even killed, because bystanders did not want to "get involved." These may be extreme cases, but a similar refusal to get involved with others often manifests itself in failure to say a kind word, to extend a helping hand, to show some tangible sign of understanding and concern, even when the other person is a friend or associate.

Intimacy, as I have described it, obviously involves the risk of self-sacrifice. That should not be surprising. As we have seen, any intimate encounter—with God, with a fellow human being or with oneself—is dangerous, for it can demand radical changes of us. It can shake us from our lethargy and require us to make peace with God, our neighbor and even ourselves. To reach out and relate to others in a way that fosters well-being and growth in them and us requires courage and self-discipline. One risks being rejected or feeling foolish. But the fruits of authentic Christian intimacy are worth the risks.

Paul is a model of such intimacy. We know from his letters that he had close human relationships:

Give my greetings to Prisca and Aquila; they were my

fellow workers in the service of Christ Jesus and even risked their lives for the sake of mine. . . . Greetings to my beloved Epaenetus; he is the first offering that Asia made to Christ. My greetings to Mary, who has worked hard for you. . . . Greetings to Ampliatus, who is dear to me in the Lord; to Urbanus, our fellow worker in the service of Christ; and to my beloved Stachys. . . .

(Romans 16:3-6, 8-7)

But the prime model for Christian intimacy is Jesus. The Gospels speak of his close relationships with many men and women. He often risked his reputation and even his life for those he loved. Eventually, he gave his life to enter into the ultimate intimacy with us—the intimacy of the Redeemer who frees us from sin, the Mediator through whom we are reestablished in God's friendship and love.

### Following Christ in Today's World

For each of us individually and for the entire human family, the Incarnation of Jesus and the risen Lord's continued presence in the world have tremendous significance. As we have seen, the Incarnation has established a new relationship not only between us and God but also among us human beings. Because he became flesh and redeemed us through his death and resurrection, the old order has passed away; now, as Paul told the Christian converts, we are a "new creation" (2 Corinthians 5:17).

Paul's language may seem poetic, but it has literal, practical meaning. Although I alluded earlier to the communitarian aspect of Christianity, I focused mainly on the individual dimension of Christian faith—how we are expected to shape our individual lives according to the gospel. Now I want to reflect on some of the implications of that new relationship with our neighbors. While outreach to others takes many forms, I shall highlight three: being "present" to friends and neighbors, helping the poor by promoting justice, and living as peacemakers. What I say is meant merely to illustrate how following the Lord Jesus leads one to become involved in these and other social issues.

*Presence to others.* In order to be "present" to others Jesus gave of himself; so must we. Many people today are suffering, have empty lives, search vainly for meaning. We find them all around us: They may include members of our families, our closest friends, people with whom we work. We see this emptiness and despair, for example, in a betrayed spouse; in a person whose zest for life has been eroded by serious illness or loneliness; in those who have lost control over their destiny because of drugs or drinking; in those whom life's difficulties and disappointments have made cynical or bitter; in those on the verge of despair because the material values in which they placed their trust have failed them.

As believers in the Lord Jesus, people intimately united with the Lord who have experienced his love, mercy and forgiveness, we can bring joy, consolation and hope to those who are suffering. We cannot remove all the pain and frustration which are part of the human condition. But we can help people cope better with their trials by encouraging them to see their sufferings in the light of the Transcendent, which assures them that a new and better life exists beyond this vale of tears, and to find meaning in their suffering here and now by identifying themselves with the sufferings of Christ (cf. Colossians 1:24).[10]

Something I said on another occasion to priests applies, I believe, to all Christians. Usually, what people need and want from us is much less difficult to discern and give than we tend to suppose. People do not expect solutions to all their problems or answers to all their questions. Often they know the answers already, or know that their problems have no immediate solutions. But more than anything else, people look to us—to you and to me—for our *presence* as loving, caring and forgiving persons. They want our help in their efforts to handle pain and frustration. They turn to us for understanding; they seek a sensitive and consoling response to their hurt feelings; they need the spiritual comfort we can bring them. They want someone who will pray with them, whose presence will remind them that, no matter what difficulties they face, God loves them, cares for them, will never abandon them. As faith-filled people who live in close union with Jesus and reflect his qualities in our lives, we can give them this assurance.

*Our obligation to the poor.* The Gospels depict Jesus' great sensitivity to the poor and oppressed. He was criticized for openly associating with them and acting as their advocate. Fidelity to his teaching and example demands that we show the same concern for the poor and suffering people of our day by promoting justice. In times of economic crisis, for example, we must not allow the heaviest burden of adjustments in social and fiscal policy to fall on those least able to help themselves. We must seek to have their voices heard and their needs considered in the arena of public policy.

This was the thrust of Pope John Paul's message to the American people in his homily at the Mass in Yankee Stadium in 1979:

> Social thinking and social practice inspired by the gospel must always be marked by a special sensitivity toward those who are most in distress, those who are extremely poor, those suffering from all the physical, mental and moral ills that afflict humanity, including hunger, neglect, unemployment and despair.

The Pope made it clear that such sensitivity (which the Latin American bishops have described as a "preferential option" for the poor) is a real obligation. It is a matter of justice and not simply of charity:

> The poor in the United States and of the world are your brothers and sisters in Christ. You must never be content to leave them just the crumbs from the feast. You must take of your substance, and not just of your abundance, in order to help them. And you must treat them like guests at your family table.[11]

The reality of poverty in the world at large and even in our wealthy United States is startling and scandalous. For its victims, poverty means ignorance, helplessness, fear, hunger, illness and even death. Poverty erodes human dignity by withholding the conditions which make it possible for people to live in dignity and self-respect. How those of us who do not suffer from this scourge respond to the poor is a test of our humanity and also of our Christianity.

There is a sense in which we need the poor in our

lives. I do not mean this in an exploitative sense—not even the subtly exploitative "Lady Bountiful" sense which views the poor as fortunate beneficiaries of our largesse. I mean instead that we need the poor to challenge our complacency and selfishness, to force us to open our eyes and our hearts, which we might not otherwise do. Faced with the fact of poverty, we must acknowledge the sinful structures and systems which oppress people and set about correcting them. Faced with the poor themselves, we must cultivate a spirit of sharing, generosity, hospitality and service, and put it into action through appropriate, personal deeds.

*The quest for peace.* The gospels portray Jesus as a man of peace. Whenever he spoke of his Kingdom, he made it clear that justice and peace were to be among its essential hallmarks. He wanted people to live together in harmony, working to build up the human family, not destroy it.

For nearly two millenia the message of the Prince of Peace has been preached to the world, yet seldom has the world enjoyed authentic peace. Today peace seems more elusive than ever. Instead of turning instruments of war into plowshares, as the Scriptures admonish us to do, nations are building not only more weapons but increasingly destructive ones.

What folly! Even as a method of deterrence, the arms race, especially the escalation of nuclear arms, is a treacherous way to preserve peace. As Pope John Paul II told the United Nations in 1979:

> The continual preparation for war, demonstrated by the production of ever more numerous, powerful and sophisticated weapons in various countries, shows that there is a desire to be ready for war, and being ready means being able to start it; it also means taking the risk that sometime, somewhere, somehow, someone can set in motion the terrible mechanism of general destruction.[12]

The Pope pleaded for a reduction in nuclear arms and their eventual elimination, a plea repeated by the bishops of the United States in their pastoral letter on war and peace.

In light of all this, there is a moral imperative for nations to do everything possible to prevent any use of nuclear weapons under any conditions. But why speak only of "nations"? As Christians and citizens, we are obliged to do all we can to create a climate conducive to ending the arms race and eliminating all nuclear weapons and other weapons of massive destructive force. No opportunity must be lost to take those steps, no matter how small, which will halt humankind's rush toward self-destruction.

It is true that nations have a right to defend themselves and that national leaders must be prudent in safeguarding their people's interests. But the interests of nations and peoples today require leaving no stone unturned in the search for peace. Let us reject the idea that the only, or the best, way to peace is through unremitting preparation for war. Let us seek urgently for alternatives to war as a means of resolving conflicts and injustices. Not to do so would be immoral negligence.

To speak of social issues may seem to have little to do with the theme of prayer and participation in the Church's sacramental life as bases for our relationship with Jesus. But there is a direct and necessary connection. As prayer and the sacraments are the foundation of our relationship with Jesus, so that relationship is—or should be—the ground and context for our lives, including our efforts to address and remedy the social evils of our times.

I have said of prayer—and could as well say of participation in the sacraments—that if it is authentic it leads, among other things, to a clearer understanding and more wholehearted acceptance of one's personal vocation, and so to greater knowledge of self and greater intimacy with others. Loving the Lord and living in communion with him have a profound effect on our personal growth and our relationships. While growth in sanctity—which comes about preeminently through prayer and the sacraments—is an interior phenomenon, it is inseparable from how we live and manifest love for others.

Paul describes the manifestation of Christian love in these words:

> Love is patient; love is kind. Love is not jealous, it does not put on airs, it is not snobbish. Love is never rude, it is not self-seeking, it is not prone to anger; neither does it brood over injuries. Love does not rejoice in what is

wrong but rejoices with the truth. There is no limit to love's forbearance, to its trust, its hope, its power to endure. Love never fails. (1 Corinthians 13:4-8)

True, love of this kind is oriented to heavenly fulfillment, but it also has the power to change the world. If we only tried to love consistently in this way, our families, our communities, our places of work and recreation and indeed all our enterprises would be well on the way to becoming models of Christ's love and peace, witnesses before the entire world of how people who accept Christ's lordship live together in mutual respect and love.

Perhaps this sounds like a simple, even simplistic, solution to the many complex problems of families, communities, nations and the world at large. I do not mean to be simplistic. Certainly the solutions required call for much thought, skill and hard work—they must be as complex and sophisticated as the problems. In the final analysis, however, sophistication, skill, hard work and the rest will accomplish very little to change the world or our lives—lastingly and for the better, at least—unless they are energized and directed by the power of love. And we best learn to love in prayer and the sacraments, by turning to love's model and source—Jesus, who is Love.

# Conclusion

**J**esus himself is the supreme model and best guide for living the Christian life. But we also need and seek other guides and models—men and women who, in their own times and places, responding to their own personal vocations, showed what it means to follow Christ. These men and women are the saints. Preeminent among them is Mary.

One cannot speak long about Jesus without speaking of his Mother. It saddens me to hear, as I sometimes do, that mistaken notions of "renewal" have diminished her role in the lives of Christians. It is sad, too, to hear it said that this is somehow what Vatican Council II had in mind. Do people who say this really know what the Council said about Mary? It spoke of her in its most important document, the *Dogmatic Constitution on the Church*, precisely in order to bring into sharper focus her role in the Church and, therefore, the ecclesial significance of devotion to her.

Only in the context of the Incarnation, which expresses God's unbelievable love for us, can we really understand Mary's role and her greatness. It is right that we extol Mary and her many privileges, but not in isolation from the mystery of Christ and the Church. Unfortunately, the latter tendency sometimes existed in the past. The Council sought to correct that by situating Marian doctrine and devotion very clearly in God's plan of salvation.

When this is done, we see more clearly Mary's place in relation to the central doctrines of the Incarnation and Redemption. Quite simply, her relationship to Jesus becomes much clearer, and we perceive how Mary's various titles or prerogatives illuminate the one fundamental truth of God in Christ. For example, her title of *theotokos* (the one who gives birth to God) is rightly understood and treated in relation to Christology; the setting for the dogma of the Immaculate Conception becomes the doctrine of grace and redemption, of which it is an element; the title "Virgin" is seen from the viewpoint of a theology of covenant; and the dogma of the Assumption is viewed from the perspective of Christian eschatology, telling us not only of Mary's destiny but of ours. Mariological doctrine, like Christological doctrine, is not abstract but is intensely related to Christian life.

Aside from the theological significance of Mary and her role in the plan of salvation, there is also a very important practical consideration bearing upon an authentic appreciation of and devotion to the Blessed Virgin: Mary has a great deal to say to us now in our contemporary setting, because she is an outstanding model for a Christ-centered spirituality.

It has been said that all spirituality, no matter what specific form it takes, is ultimately Marian. When I first heard that, I was somewhat startled. But upon reflection, it makes much sense. For what do we mean by spirituality? What is its basis? In the final analysis, all spirituality is rooted in the fundamental orientation of the individual and the community to the demands which the gospel makes—namely, that we hear and accept the Word and manifest the glory of the Word in our lives. Of all human persons, Mary has done this most perfectly; her spirituality is thus the model for the entire Church.

The incident in Luke's Gospel where Gabriel told Mary of God's plan for her bears this out. In response she asked: "How can this be since I do not know man?" I do not think this expresses doubt or hesitation, but only a reasonable human desire to understand. When she learned that she would conceive by the Holy Spirit, Mary had no more questions. "I am the servant of the Lord," she said. "Let it be done to me as you say" (Luke 1:34, 38). Because Mary heard God's word and responded to it, the Word became incarnate in her.

Shortly afterwards, she hastened to visit her cousin Elizabeth, who had also conceived a child in extraordinary circumstances. On that occasion Mary sang her song of praise in which she testified to the power of God's Word in her:

"My being proclaims the greatness of the Lord,
    my spirit finds joy in God my savior,
For he has looked upon his servant in her lowliness;
    all ages to come shall call me blessed." (Luke 1:46-48)

Mary truly heard the Word, allowed it to become incarnate in her and witnessed to its glory and power in her life. That is why she is the model for our own relationship with the Word. Like Mary, we must see the Word not as something external to us but as the most profound mystery in our lives. Like Mary, too, we must cherish this mystery within us as a precious gift which God gives us not only for our own personal well-being but for that of the entire human family.

I encourage you to read and prayerfully reflect on the late Pope Paul VI's *Apostolic Exhortation on Marian Devotion.* In this wonderful document the Holy Father explained why Mary's example is so relevant to the contemporary Church:

> The Virgin Mary has always been proposed to the faithful by the Church as an example to be imitated, not precisely in the type of life she led, and much less for the socio-cultural background in which she lived and which today scarcely exists anywhere. She is held up as an example to the faithful rather for the way in which, in her own particular life, she fully and responsibly accepted the will of God, because she heard the word of God and acted on it, and because charity and a spirit of service were the driving force of her actions. She is worthy of imitation because she was the first and most perfect of Christ's disciples.[13]

Mary is a wonderful model and a source of inspiration for us as we seek to meet the challenges of today's Church and society. She did not run away from life and its demands. She accepted life freely and eagerly. She stood up, declared herself and made decisions. Never in the history of the human family has there been a freer, more responsible and more far-reaching decision than Mary's acceptance of the invitation to be the Mother of the Savior.

So we can truly say, as Pope Paul VI did, that Mary was a perfect Christian whose example can give direction, strength and inspiration to our efforts to respond to the Lord's call. Indeed, I believe it is correct to say that Mary's true greatness rests not so much on the privileges and honors which were bestowed on her in virtue of her special calling—and which we have no reason to expect for ourselves—as on her own free, generous and unreserved acceptance of God's will—which we have at least some capacity for emulating.

Our Catholic tradition has always given a prominent place to Mary. From the very beginning, we have taken to heart that wonderful woman who gave her flesh to our Savior and who, together with her husband Joseph, nurtured and cared for him during his early years. There is no doubt that she loved her son intensely and that he loved her. To be close to Jesus we must have a special place in our hearts for her. There is no other way.

Earlier I spoke of the significance of the Incarnation in its implications for us personally. In the intimate relationship between Mary and Jesus we see better than any other the communion of the divine and the human. No relationship this side of heaven tells us as much about God's love and tenderness toward the human family. And it is the model of our own intimacy with the Lord!

## The Fondness of God

Father Edward Farrell, a well-known spiritual writer, begins one of his books with a touching story. A priest visiting Ireland some years ago was walking one evening along a country road near the place where he was staying. He met an old man who also was out for an evening stroll. They walked and talked together until a sudden shower caused them to take shelter nearby. As they waited for the rain to stop, they continued chatting for a while, but finally they ran out of conversation. The old Irishman took out his little prayerbook and began to pray, half aloud. The priest watched him for a long time. Then quietly he said, "You must be very close to God." The old man simply smiled and, without embarrassment or self-consciousness, answered, "Yes, he is very fond of me." That reply became the title of Father Farrell's book: *The Father Is Very Fond of Me.*[14]

Indeed, the Father is very fond of us all—so fond that he could not bear for us to be separated from him. He therefore sent his Son to redeem us. Through his death and resurrection, Jesus offers us a new kind of life, radically different from the life of unredeemed humanity. As Paul told the Corinthians:

> [Christ] died for all so that those who live might live no longer for themselves, but for him who for their sakes died and was raised up.... If anyone is in Christ, he is a new creation. The old order has passed away; now all is new! (2 Corinthians 5:15,17)

In this pastoral reflection I have tried to say what this new life means to us in practice, what actually happens to us when we accept Jesus in faith and turn over our lives to him. As I conclude, I wish to do three things.

First, I want to profess my faith in the Lord Jesus and all that he has taught us. I believe in the Lord, and I wish to love him with all my mind and heart and soul. The great desire of my life—one which becomes stronger as I grow older—is to be intimately united with him so that I can experience in the very depth of my being his great love for me, so that his life will be mine.

I understand, of course, that this will not happen without effort on my part. I must avoid those things which separate me from the Lord. When I sin, I must repent and seek forgiveness. I must always follow the Lord's example, trying each day to shape my life and ministry according to his. I must constantly seek to grow spiritually, to develop an ever greater intimacy with him through personal prayer, through participation in the Church's sacramental life and through my ministry—especially to the poor and forgotten people of the world. I must work tirelessly to proclaim Jesus and his gospel to the entire human family.

I know very well that, because of human weakness, I do not always measure up to what is expected of me. As I said in the beginning of this pastoral letter, my failures cause me pain and frustration. Still, like Paul, I do not despair or give up, for I know the Lord loves me and will never abandon me. He will make his strength mine if I let him. I take this occasion to reaffirm my faith and my determination to place myself totally in the hands of the Lord.

Second, I wish to affirm and encourage you as you

search for the Lord and seek to grow in intimacy with him. Do you ever feel misunderstood, lonely, discouraged, wounded, abandoned? So did he, and there is meaning in our painful experiences when we understand and accept them as a way of sharing in his sufferings. More than that, in our moments of pain we can and should turn to him as a friend. What other friend has won for us victory over death itself? He is very close to us, only waiting for us to turn and place ourselves in his hands so that he can help us.

Mark's Gospel tells of a man whom Jesus cured of leprosy. The leper put himself at Jesus' mercy and asked to be cured. Mark tells us: "Moved with pity, Jesus stretched out his hand, touched him, and said, 'I do will it. Be cured'" (Mark 1:41).

You and I are like that leper. We are spiritually ill, and we need to be healed. Often we are reluctant—even afraid—to approach Jesus. Will he understand? We have sinned so often—will he believe the sincerity of our repentance now? I urge you to put aside such embarrassment and anxiety. Place yourself at his mercy and he will take pity on you, touch you, heal you. He will shower on you his love and understanding. He will pierce through the dark cloud hanging over you, so that, seeing the radiance of his glory and saving power, you can take heart.

Finally, I ask you to join me in prayer for all those who are not close to the Lord, the many people who desperately need to experience his love but who, for whatever reason, have not sought his mercy. They are all around us: perhaps a spouse or child, another relative or a friend, a neighbor or fellow worker. Pray that they will have the courage to reach out to Jesus and experience his healing power. And to our prayer let us join personal gestures of love and concern, since often it is through us that Jesus wishes to reveal himself to others, using us as instruments to mediate his saving graces.

Together we are called to do the work of the Lord. May the love, joy, peace and hope which are the fruits of fidelity to Jesus be with us always. I make Paul's prayer for the Ephesians my own prayer for you:

I pray that [the Father] will bestow on you gifts in keeping with the riches of his glory. May he strengthen you inwardly through the working of his Spirit. May Christ dwell in your hearts through faith, and may charity be the root and foundation of your life. Thus you will be able to grasp fully, with all the holy ones, the breadth and length and height and depth of Christ's love, and experience this love which surpasses all knowledge, so that you may attain to the fullness of God himself. (Ephesians 3:16-19)

Your brother in Christ,
Joseph Cardinal Bernardin
Archbishop of Chicago

Appendix

# The Development of Christology Today

Theologians today are actively discussing a number of Christological questions. In itself, this is healthy. But publicity and popular writing sometimes leave the impression that our basic understanding of Jesus and his mission is changing radically, that the creeds which have been such an important part of our lives no longer mean what we thought they meant. This, of course, is not so.

What, then, are the theologians doing? What is the purpose of their research and writing? What is their relationship to the Church's magisterium and the bishops?

### Bishops and Theologians: A Creative Tension

Let me begin with the last question first. The bishop bears the responsibility for presenting the teachings and the person of Christ to the people of God in his own diocese and to the world at large. In part, this implies ensuring that the contents of revelation remain undistorted by any human error. Together with the Holy Father and all the bishops, he has final authority over what is presented as the teaching of the Church.

Another aspect of the bishop's role as a teacher is to cultivate an ever-increasing understanding of divine revelation. For this reason the bishop must encourage and promote further study and deeper penetration of God's Word to us as well as better formulations of God's truth in the context of contemporary social and intellectual realities. In other words, while the bishop's responsibility is to see that the basic content of the revelation remains constant, he must also see that it is pertinent and meaningful to his people.[15]

The bishop carries out his responsibility to further penetrate the meaning of revelation primarily through promoting study and reflection by theologians. They look to the past, they look to present realities, they look to future possibilities in order to provide a deeper understanding of what God is saying to us. In the vast region of God's message to us, they are the explorers.

Because their work implies searching, they must have a certain amount of freedom. At the same time, we must expect that their searches will not always be successful, that there are going to be some mistakes. In conducting these explorations, however, the theologian provides a great and necessary service to the Church. The theologian keeps the Church intellectually alive, in touch with the realities of the world in which it exists, as well as in touch with its own roots and basic realities.

Insofar as theologians are dealing with revealed truth, they are subject to the judgment and the teaching of the Church's bishops. What this means, in essence, is that there must be collaboration, cooperation and support among theologians and bishops. There is a necessary creative tension built into this relationship, and through it the Church continues to grow in her witness to Christ.

### Developments in Biblical Studies

To explain what contemporary theologians are doing and what the purpose of their research is, it is first necessary to understand that the way in which we study the Bible has undergone significant developments in recent decades.

After the Council of Trent, Catholic biblical studies were primarily apologetic in character—that is, focused on defending the biblical origin of Catholic dogma. From the middle of the last century, however, biblical scholars have developed more learned and scientific approaches to the Scriptures. For the most part, the purpose of these new methods of interpretation has been to grasp the meaning of biblical texts in light of their literary, historical and canonical contexts. Of special importance for this task has been the discovery of the function of various literary forms or genres in ancient Jewish and Christian literature.

Although the Church was understandably hesitant

about new methods of interpreting the sacred texts of Scripture, Pope Leo XIII and Pope Benedict XV wrote encyclicals encouraging biblical studies and providing guidelines for scholars.[16] The Pontifical Biblical Commission was established in 1902 to oversee these developments. In 1943 Pope Pius XII, in his encyclical *Divino Afflante Spiritu,* gave a major impetus to scientific biblical studies, initiating a new era in Catholic exegesis.

Another important development took place in 1964 when the Pontifical Biblical Commission issued an *Instruction on the Historical Truth of the Gospels.*[17] It counseled Catholic biblical scholars to use the historical critical method as well as form criticism with circumspection in order to gain a fuller understanding of the Gospels.

In 1965 the Second Vatican Council promulgated its *Constitution on Divine Revelation.* This document made two important points which provide a framework for the work of Catholic biblical scholars. First, the Council reaffirmed what Pius XII had said in *Divino Afflante Spiritu* about the importance of distinguishing literary forms as a way of determining the intention of the human author of a biblical text: "... the interpreter of Sacred Scripture, in order to see clearly what God wanted to communicate to us, should carefully investigate what meaning the sacred writers really intended, and what God wanted to manifest by means of their words. Those who search out the intention of the sacred writers must, among other things, have regard for 'literary forms.' For truth is proposed and expressed in a variety of ways, depending on whether a text is history of one kind or another, or whether its form is that of prophecy, poetry, or some other type of speech."[18]

The other point made by the Council was that the responsibility for the final judgment about how Scripture should be interpreted rests with the official teaching authority of the Church. "The task of authentically interpreting the Word of God, whether written or handed on," the *Constitution on Divine Revelation* stated, "has been entrusted exclusively to the living teaching office of the Church, where authority is exercised in the name of Jesus Christ. This teaching office is not above the Word of God, but serves it, teaching only what has been handed on, listening to it devoutly, guarding it scrupulously, and explaining it faithfully by divine commission and with the help of the Holy Spirit; it draws from this one deposit of faith everything which it presents for belief as divinely revealed."[19]

It is within the framework of these norms that biblical scholars and theologians are to probe anew the mystery of Christ, not in order to change what we believe about Jesus but to enrich our understanding and belief. They are studying the revelation about Jesus in the Scriptures and his universal significance for the human family.

## Questions in Contemporary Christology

This brings us back to the question posed earlier: What is the meaning of contemporary biblical and theological study about Christ? This can best be answered by focusing on six questions in contemporary Christology.

*1) The meaning of the "historical" Jesus.* Using all available biblical methods, it is important that we find out all we can about the "historical" Jesus, the God-man who lived and died in a concrete geographical, cultural, religious and historical setting. The primary goal of this research, however, is to discover the *meaning* of Jesus for humanity.

The Scriptures situate the life and mission of Jesus in the larger context of God's plan of salvation. The evangelists are less concerned about providing *historical details* about his life than presenting, under divine inspiration, a *theological understanding* of his ministry, death and resurrection. As the International Theological Commission stated:

> The New Testament does not intend to convey mere historical information concerning Jesus. It seeks above all to hand down the witness which ecclesial faith bears concerning Jesus and to present him in the fulness of his significance as 'Christ' (Messiah) and as 'Lord' (Kyrios, God). This witness is an expression of faith, and seeks to elicit faith. A 'biography' of Jesus in the modern sense of this word cannot be produced, if it were taken to entail a precise and detailed account.[20]

It would be wrong to suppose that research is needed to discover the "real" Jesus as though we had not known him up to now. Rather, as the Theological Commission says, there is a "substantive and radical unity" between the historical Jesus and the Christ of faith, a unity which "pertains to the very essence of the Gospel message."[21] The Jesus of history is also the Jesus whom we know in our creeds and celebrate in our liturgy. Historical research on Jesus, understood correctly, does not undermine Christological dogma but deepens our knowledge of Jesus and enhances our acceptance of him in faith.

*2) Restating Christological truths.* Another aim of the current renewal in Christology is to address difficulties which dogmatic statements of the early councils can present for people today because of their language or the philosophical concepts they employ. Not only do the dogmatic statements themselves pose such a difficulty, so does subsequent theology which was itself aimed at a better understanding of the dogmatic statements and their implications.

During the first several centuries of the Church, there were a number of serious Christological controversies. Basically, they arose from the effort to explain how Jesus could be both fully divine and fully human, with the exception of sin. Some explanations were heretical because they ended by denying Christ's divinity (for example, Arianism). At other times the error lay in undermining or denying the full humanity of Jesus (for example, Gnosticism and Docetism).

Several ecumenical councils dealt with these controversies. In dialogue with one another, they reshaped Christological terms and definitions. The Council of Nicea (325 A.D.) affirmed Christ's divinity by defining that the Son is consubstantial (*homoousios*) with the Father. The Council of Ephesus (431 A.D.) affirmed the real unity of the divine and human natures in the person of Christ. The Council of Chalcedon (451 A.D.), in an effort to uphold Jesus' humanity, considered how both the divine and human natures can be united in one person. It stated that the two natures exist within the person of Christ:

> Following therefore the holy Fathers, we unanimously
> teach and confess one and the same Son, our Lord Jesus
> Christ, the same perfect in divinity and perfect in

humanity, the same truly God and truly man composed of rational soul and body, the same one in being (*homoousios*) with the Father as to divinity and one in being with us as to humanity, like unto us in all things but sin.... The same was begotten from the Father before the ages as to the divinity and in the latter days for us and for our salvation was born as to his humanity from Mary the Virgin Mother of God.

We confess that one and the same Lord Jesus Christ, the only-begotten son, must be acknowledged in two natures, without confusion or change, without division or separation. The distinction between the natures was never abolished by their union but ather the character proper to each of the two natures was preserved as they came together in one person (*prosopon*) and one hypostasis. He is not split or divided into two persons but he is one and the same only-begotten, God the Word, the Lord Jesus Christ, as formerly the prophets and later Jesus Christ himself have taught us about him and as has been handed down to us by the Symbol of the Fathers.[22]

Several other important Christological councils followed Chalcedon. While firmly rooted in the teaching of the Fathers of the Church and the Councils of Nicea, Constantinople, Ephesus and Chalcedon, they clarified a number of questions which had arisen. In doing so, they further enriched the Church's understanding of Christ and his meaning for the human family. The Third Council of Constantinople (681 A.D.), in particular, gave a "better perception of the place occupied in the salvation of mankind by the humanity of Christ, and by the various 'mysteries' of his life on earth, such as his baptism, his temptations and the 'agony' of Gethsemani."[23]

Contemporary difficulties with the dogmatic statements of these councils do not concern the *truth* they convey, which can never change, but some of the philosophical terms and concepts they use. For example, words such as *substance, nature* and *person* are not generally understood by people today in the same sense in which they were used by the early Council Fathers. Theologians are, therefore, attempting to restate the Christological truths in language and concepts which are understood and accepted today. The main concern is "to show how the dogma 'true God and true man in one person' was to be understood in faith today, and how it could be interpreted and adapted with the aid of modern philosophical methods and categories."[24]

This is laudable. The International Theological Commission states: "As history takes its course, and cultural changes occur, the teachings of the Council of Chalcedon and Constantinople III must always be actualized in the consciousness and preaching of the Church, under the guidance of the Holy Spirit." This, it adds, is "an obligation binding both upon the theologians and upon the apostolic solicitude of shepherds and faithful."[25] But great care must be taken to ensure that the essential truth contained in the dogmatic formulations is not changed. Therefore, both biblical scholars and theologians must be sensitive to the teaching authority of the Church, which was instituted by Christ and is assisted by his Spirit in its work of ensuring fidelity to revelation.

*3) Jesus and his mission.* In the past, Christology has sometimes focused more on the person of Christ than on his mission (soteriology). As a result, Jesus' person and his work tended to be separated in people's minds.[26] One aim of modern Christology, therefore, is to examine more deeply Christ's mission and his ministry. This will enrich our understanding of Christ and his meaning for us.

The International Theological Commission has expressed support for this effort to bring about a better synthesis of the person of Jesus and his work of redemption. "Some theological speculations," it said, "have failed to adequately preserve this intimate connection between Christology and soteriology. Today, it is always imperative to seek ways to better express the reciprocity of these two aspects of the saving event which is itself undivided."[27]

*4) Christ's pre-existence.* As the earthly life of Jesus has been examined rather closely in modern Christological research, this has led to a reexamination of his pre-existence (the person who becomes human as Jesus Christ was always in existence beforehand) and the role that reality plays in the New Testament and early Church Fathers.

63

The International Theological Commission has also addressed this issue. After referring to Jesus' resurrection, the Commission states, "In the light of this exaltation the origin of Jesus Christ is openly and definitively understood: sitting at the right hand of God in his post-existence (that is, after his earthly life) implies his pre-existence with God from the beginning before he came into the world."[28]

The same report goes on to say, "Jesus Christ's origin from the Father is not a conclusion of subsequent reflection but is made clear by his words and the facts about him, namely that Jesus took it for certain that he had been sent by the Father."[29] Later the Commission acknowledges that "the concept of the pre-existence of Jesus Christ has acquired greater clarity as Christological reflection has evolved."[30]

*5) Searching for a compassionate God.* Closer attention to the Scriptures and especially to the doctrine of the Cross has led us more deeply into another mystery of our faith. The Scriptures often speak of God's "suffering" or of his "compassion." In the New Testament we encounter a Jesus who weeps, who gets angry and who feels sadness. How are these expressions to be understood in the light of doctrine about God's immutability (his unchangeableness) and his impassibility (being beyond the reach of suffering)?

The International Theological Commission has stated that affirming God's impassibility "is not to be understood as though God remained indifferent to human events. God loves us with the love of friendship, and he wishes to be loved by us in return. When this love is offended, Sacred Scripture speaks of suffering on the part of God. On the other hand, it speaks of his joy when the sinner is converted." It goes on to say, "there is undoubtedly something worth retaining in the expressions of Holy Scripture and the Fathers, as well as in some recent theologies, even though they require clarification."[31] This fits in well with our contemporary desire and search for a God who is all-powerful but also compassionate towards us in our sufferings, a God who in some way suffers with us.[32]

*6) Jesus' knowledge.* A number of themes and issues in contemporary Christology come together in discussion of a question which has received a good deal of recent scholarly and popular attention: the question of Jesus' knowledge. There are several dimensions to this question. One relates to his knowledge of the ordinary affairs of life: his knowledge of religious matters (for example, of the Scriptures and contemporary religious concepts) and his knowledge of the future (for example, of his passion, death and resurrection, the destruction of Jerusalem, the Parousia or Second Coming). The other dimension, in a sense more sensitive and important, is Jesus' awareness or consciousness of himself as Messiah, Son of God, and of his salvific mission.

Our questions about Jesus' human knowledge and human consciousness of his unique relationship to the Father stem from the fact that he is truly man as well as God. In his humanity, he was like us in everything except sin. As the letter to the Hebrews states: "... therefore he had to become like his brothers in every way that he might be a merciful and faithful high priest before God on their behalf, to expiate the sins of the people. Since he was himself tested through what he suffered, he is able to help those who are tempted" (2:17-18).

That being the case, how could he have had knowledge of all things from the very beginning of his earthly existence? In what sense are we to understand Luke's statement that, after his parents found him in the Temple, "Jesus, for his part, progressed steadily in wisdom and age and grace before God and men" (Luke 2:52)? Does this imply that, initially at least, he lacked full knowledge of all things, including his unique relationship to the Father and his salvific mission? If so, how do we explain that limitation, since, in the one person of Christ, his human nature is united with his divine nature (the hypostatic union)?

If, in trying to resolve this problem, unlimited knowledge is attributed to Jesus (because of his superlative gifts and mission), one might fail to respect the truth of Jesus' real share in our limited humanness. But, by going too far in the other direction and denying all special knowledge in Jesus, one might fail to respect the exigencies of his mission and the reality of his gifts as a prophet.

For many centuries the Church has held that Jesus had unlimited knowledge. In order to explain how Jesus, even in his humanity, had unlimited knowledge, the theologians of the Middle Ages attributed to him different types of extraordinary knowledge including *beatific knowledge* (in his immediate vision of the Word the human soul of Jesus knew all that God knows and knew it in the same way in which God knows it) and *infused knowledge* (Jesus' intellect was gifted with special knowledge from God similar to the knowledge traditionally attributed to angels).

In this century there have been several official Church pronouncements concerning Christ's knowledge. In 1918, for example, the Holy Office declared as "unsafe" for teaching in Catholic seminaries and universities the opinion that Christ may not have had the beatific vision during his lifetime, that he would not have known "from the beginning ... everything, past, present and future, that is to say, everything which God knows with the knowledge of vision."[33]

In 1943 Pope Pius XII declared in his encyclical on *The Church as the Mystical Body of Christ* (*Mystici Corporis*) that Jesus enjoyed the beatific vision "from the time he was received into the womb of the Mother of God." Consequently, "the loving knowledge with which the divine Redeemer has pursued us from the first moment of his Incarnation is such as completely to surpass all the searchings of the human mind."[34]

With the new era in biblical studies initiated by Pius XII in 1943, Catholic scholars have made an intense effort to come to a better knowledge of the historical Christ. Understandably, this effort has focused attention again on the question of Christ's human knowledge. The International Theological Commission has supported this. "Theologians," it said, "must also devote their full attention to perennially difficult questions: for example, the questions relative to the consciousness and knowledge of Christ...."[35] More recently, the Commission has indicated a hope to bring this issue to a satisfactory conclusion.[36]

From what has been described above, it should be clear that the theological endeavors of orthodox and responsible scholars about Christological questions are not intended to downplay or deny either Jesus' divinity or his humanity. Rather, the precise intent of scientific scriptural interpretation and theological reflection is to probe and ground the revealed truth believed and taught by the Church: that in the one person Jesus Christ the divine and human natures are united without confusion or division.

These efforts by scholars are not infallible; they can be one-sided and they can be mistaken. But they are aimed at helping us understand better the mystery of Christ, the God-man. Ultimately, of course, to be sure that efforts to understand the mystery of Jesus do not deviate from the truth God has revealed, faithful Catholics, scholars and non-scholars alike, seek guidance from and are faithful to the magisterium.

In the latter months of 1984, the Pontifical Biblical Commission published a document, *Bible et Christologie,* to guide Christological research.[37] It first examines eleven contemporary approaches to the biblical text, pointing out the advantages of each as well as their limitations. The second part is a brief summary of biblical witnesses relevant to Christology, including the expectations of salvation and of a Messiah (in the First or Old Testament) and their fulfillment in Jesus Christ (in the New Testament). The document insists on the importance of moving toward an integral Christology which includes promise and fulfillment and takes into consideration the totality of the biblical witnesses to Jesus the Christ. Biblical scholars and theologians will find valuable guidance in this latest document from the Holy See.

The relationship between the magisterium and theologians is one of mutuality. Theologians look to the magisterium for guidance. The teaching authority of the Church, through such vehicles as the International Theological Commission and the Pontifical Biblical Commission, responds to the work of theologians and biblical scholars and evaluates them in the light of the Church's traditions regarding faith and morals.

The goal—understanding the mystery of Jesus—will never be fully achieved in this life. In the meantime, however, theological reflection is an exciting endeavor, one that can deepen our faith and bring us closer to Jesus, God's only Son.

## Footnotes

1. *Dogmatic Constitution on the Church (Lumen Gentium), The Documents of Vatican II,* 1964, #9.

2. Pope John Paul II, *The Redeemer of Man (Redemptor Hominis)* 1979, #13.

3. St. Augustine, *Confessions.*

4. Pope John Paul II, Address to Mexican Bishops in Puebla de Los Angeles, Mexico, January 28, 1979. *Messages of John Paul II* (Daughters of St. Paul, 1979), p. 261.

5. Robert Bolt, *A Man for All Seasons* (New York: Random House, 1962).

6. Joseph L. Bernardin, Address to the National Conference of Catholic Bishops, November 14, 1977.

7. *Instruction on Eucharistic Worship,* 1967, #3; cf. also the "General Instruction" of the new *Sacramentary,* 1974, #1-15.

8. *Constitution on the Sacred Liturgy (Sacrosanctum Concilium), The Documents of Vatican II,* 1963.

9. *Ibid.,* #10.

10. Cf. Pope John Paul II, *Apostolic Letter on the Christian Meaning of Human Suffering (Salvifici Doloris),* February 11, 1984.

11. Pope John Paul II, "Open Wide the Doors for Christ," Homily for Mass in Yankee Stadium, New York, October 2, 1979, *U.S.A. The Message of Justice, Peace and Love,* (Daughters of St. Paul, 1979).

12. Pope John Paul II, Address to the XXXIV General Assembly of the United Nations Organization, October 2, 1979, *ibid.*

13. Pope Paul VI, *Apostolic Exhortation on Marian Devotion (Marialis Cultus),* February 2, 1974.

14. Cf. Edward Farrell, *The Father Is Very Fond of Me* (Foreword), (Denville, N.J.: Dimension Books, 1975).

15. Cf. *Dogmatic Constitution on the Church,* #25, and *Decree on the Bishops' Pastoral Office in the Church,* #11-13, in *The Documents of Vatican II* (1966).

16. Leo XIII, *Providentissimus Deus* (1893), and Benedict XV, *Spiritus Paraclitus* (1920).

17. *Catholic Biblical Quarterly,* vol. 26 (1964), pp. 305-312.

18. *Constitution on Divine Revelation,* #12, in *The Documents of Vatican II,* (1966).

19. *Ibid.,* #10.

20. International Theological Commission, *Select Questions on Christology* (USCC Publications, 1980), p. 2.

21. *Ibid.,* p. 3.

22. Quoted in Richard P. McBrien, *Catholicism* (Minneapolis: Winston Press, 1981), p. 456.

23. International Theological Commission, p. 8.

24. W. Kasper, *Jesus the Christ* (New York: Paulist Press, 1976), p. 17.

25. International Theological Commission, p. 11.

26. Father Gerald O'Collins, S.J., states: "Two often Christology simply lapsed into a mass of abstract and cliche burdened teachings about the divine-human constitution of Christ. It simply slipped out of view that not just 'Saviour' but all the other titles used of Jesus in the New Testament express aspirations for salvation. It was likewise forgotten that behind the Christological statements of the early Church we find soteriological themes." *What Are They Saying about Jesus?* (New York: Paulist Press, 1977), p. 11.

27. International Theological Commission, p. 12.

28. International Theological Commission, *Theology, Christology, Anthropology* (USCC Publications, 1983), p. 14.

29. *Ibid.*

30. *Ibid.,* p. 16.

31. *Ibid.,* pp. 19-20.

32. Cf. John Paul II in his Apostolic Letter, *Salvifici Doloris,* #16: "In his messianic activity in the midst of Israel, Christ drew increasingly closer to the world of human suffering ... above all ... through the fact of having taken this suffering upon his very self."

33. Denziger-Schonmetzer, *Enchiridion,* ed. XXXVI, pp. 3645, 3646.

34. Pope Pius XII, *Mystici Corporis;* Denzinger-Schonmetzer, p. 3812.

35. International Theological Commission (1980), p. 11.

36. International Theological Commission (1983), p. 13.

37. Pontifical Biblical Commission, *Bible et Christologie* (Paris: Les Editions du Cerf, 1984).